I salute the supreme teacher, the Truth, whose nature is bliss,
who is the giver of the highest happiness, who is pure wisdom,
who is beyond all qualities and infinite like the sky, who is
beyond words, who is one and eternal, pure and still, who is
beyond all change and phenomena and who is the silent witness
to all our thoughts and emotions—I salute Truth, the supreme teacher.

ANCIENT VEDIC HYMN

CONTENTS

ACKNOWLEDGMENTS

I AM GRATEFUL TO GOD for this path I've been given and for the will and tenacity it has taken to complete this project. I give special thanks to all the clients and students who have entrusted me with their wounded souls and taught me what I needed in order to write this book. May they continue to heal and grow whole.

I feel deep and eternal gratitude to the great teachers, alive and dead, who have helped me to see myself and God and to find my way in life. Without their wisdom, love, and guidance, I could never have found a solid place to stand for living my life and doing my work. Thank God that it is written in our souls that once we find our Truth, we must share it.

I am grateful to my family, the ones who helped the seed grow into the tree it is today. To Jim Fadiman, whose Sufi teaching stirred my dormant creative fires to begin this book. To Roy Eugene Davis, for his help in finding my spiritual way. To Hal Zina Bennett, for his gentle nature and for his ability to heal the soul as he edits the manuscript. To Cindy Black, Richard Cohn, and the Beyond Words staff, for their spirituality, sensitivity, and professionalism. To Aminah Raheem, for her wonderful ability to synthesize various healing techniques into one highly transformative model.

To Jim Charlton, my co-teacher all these many years, for his loving cantankerousness. To Judi Tapfer, for her soulful editing. To Anna, for my greatest of all openings. To all the friends and associates who have believed in me and encouraged my writing. And especially to my spiritual community, which has helped me discover how deep connectedness heals the soul.

And finally, a special thanks to my friend Candace, who has always believed in my spiritual and creative nature and has encouraged me to express it in every way possible.

TO THE READER

THE PEOPLE AND EVENTS in this book are real, but in most cases specific names and details have been changed. Since the subject matter is so personal and intimate, I have chosen to disclose my own life and wounds as freely as those of my clients, students, and friends. I have found this practice of self-disclosure both frightening and healing. I offer it to my readers that we may all learn to discard our masks and tell our truth.

The spiritually wounded people I describe in this book were reared in society and were wounded by its citizens and institutions. This work, however, which is about healing and wholeness, is not intended as an indictment of those individuals or institutions. Although it is difficult to identify problems without offending those who initiated them, the intention here is to stop the wounding and begin the healing. Therefore, if the words and stories in this book have cut or wounded anyone in a non-helpful manner, I deeply regret it and apologize.

I have attempted to honor the wounds of inequality that women have long suffered with the English language by using the pronouns *he* and *she* randomly and interchangeably in this book. I also debated with myself about using the name *God* as the symbol word for the Great Mystery we are redefining in this epoch, since most people associate the word with maleness. The acting industry influenced me to use the word *God* when I realized that they currently use the word *actor* to describe one of their members, female or male. I use *God* in this book in that same spirit of equality and simplicity with the intention of healing old rifts and pain. Language is a difficult taskmaster. May we all someday learn how to write, speak, and interact without causing unnecessary pain to one another.

INTRODUCTION

Discovering the Rift and the Inner Spring

URING THE DOG DAYS OF AUGUST on our farm in Ohio, in particularly dry years when all other sources of water for our cows had dried up, my brothers and I would be called upon to "dig out the spring," which was located roughly in the center of the farm. This was not a task we relished. The temperature was invariably scorching, and none of us enjoyed this backbreaking work, swinging instruments of hard labor while wading around bare to the knees in mud and cow manure, with thousands of flies clinging first to the cows, then to the cow manure, and then to our bare skin. We went and we worked, but we held the cows personally accountable for the entire affair, because we knew it was their callous indolence that set this sad state of affairs into motion.

After all, hadn't we just the year before dug out this same spring, wrangling out rocks and shoveling mud from the spring's mouth so that clear waters sprang forth again, forming a cool and inviting, rock-fringed pool from which they could drink their fill? But the cows, careless and ignorant as far as we were concerned, would invariably destroy their paradise. Engrossed in their daily industry of grazing, they would trudge through instead of around the spring toward that greener grass, occasionally dropping their ample piles of manure in the midst of it. They would run through the spring while at play or in fear, wallow in it if they were hot, and generally trample everything in and around it when drinking.

To us boys, the cows were incorrigible louts, and we were sure they worked their evil on purpose to cause work and misery for us. We credited them with extreme malice when it came to these matters that caused us misery, particularly this fouling of the spring. After all, these waters were necessary for life. What creature would randomly destroy a pure, cool spring, rendering it a mud- and shit-infested hole in the ground from which no walking creature could draw nourishment? They had to know, we concluded, that we poor boys—at great cost to health and comfort—would be forced out in the scorching heat to fix it up for them.

We hated them for it. And our drama of persecution was worsened by the fact that the cows found our work very interesting. From the start, they gathered around the spring in rows—over a hundred cows— watching us intently and occasionally mooing their impatience. "Hurry it up, suckers," we heard them say. "We want to drink our fill and then tear it all up again for you." Such cheek. Such gall. We were humiliated and couldn't wait to depart and leave these creatures to their vicious work.

This ancient scene is all a memory now. I had long forgotten it until, in the midst of my work, I stopped to ask for an image of what this book is all about for me. An image of the spring immediately came to mind. Of course, I realized, how perfect. We humans also have a clear, pure spring in the center of our beings, a spring of spirit that is our reason for being here. And we somehow lose it and befoul it just as those cows did, mindlessly in pursuit of our daily commerce, play, or some perceived crisis from without. Indeed, we are expected to do so. It is *the way of life* as we were trained to live it. Taught from infancy that we must accomplish, earn, and "become somebody," we are essentially herded away from our inner spirit, which seems to have no place in life. We become "somebody" and lose our souls.

The same happened to me in youth, and I have learned the lesson repeatedly through the years. Little did I suspect as a boy that I would be cleaning out that spring for the rest of my life, eternally helping myself and others to roll away the stones from this pure fount of life so we might drink again the waters of our soul and be restored.

I've pondered for decades the problem of the blockage to our inner spring of the soul. I've also heard many of this century's saints and sages talk about it. Mother Teresa, for example, commented more than once that the spiritual poverty in modern culture caused by our separation and isolation from God and one another is much worse than mere physical hunger and illness. This spiritual poverty makes beggars of us all, scrambling to find in the outer world the love and peace of mind that we were robbed of in the process of growing up. Mother Teresa was describing what I have grown to call *a rift with God*.

Bill, one of my students, upon returning from a visit to India, shared Mother's feelings: "I felt a great sadness in my heart," he said, "when I saw homeless families in Calcutta who had lived in the streets for generations. But the sadness was not for them. It was for me. I was reared in a wealthy but loveless household, and I still feel isolated and alone. Those street people, by contrast, were loving to one another and seemed to have a deep peace that I have never experienced. They felt truly loved and connected to one another in a way I never have. In seeing them, I recognized my own inner poverty. I felt that I was the true homeless beggar, not them. And my homelessness seemed much more destructive than simply being without a house."

The great psychologist Carl Jung, author of *Modern Man in Search of a Soul* and many other volumes, felt the same about modern culture in general, which he believed cut people off from their instincts and intuition. This was demonstrated most poignantly for him in his discussions with the indigenous peoples of Africa and America, as recalled in his book *Memories, Dreams, Reflections*. His discussions with Ochwiay Biano, a New Mexican Pueblo Indian chief, were most enlightening:

> "See," Ochwiay Biano said, "how cruel the whites look. Their lips are thin, their noses sharp, their eyes have a staring expression; they are always seeking something. What are they seeking? The whites always want something; they are always uneasy and restless. We do not know what they want. We do not understand them. We think they must be mad."
>
> I asked him why he thought the whites were all mad.
>
> "They think with their heads," he replied.
>
> Why of course, what do you think with? I asked.
>
> "We think here," he said, indicating his heart.

Jung, struck by the dignity and composure of the Hopi, concluded that it came in part from their strong spiritual beliefs and a daily ritual of communion with their mystical source:

> If we set against this our own self justifications, the meaning of our own lives as it's formulated by our reason, we cannot help but see our poverty. Out of sheer envy we are obliged to smile at the Indians' naivete and to plume ourselves on our cleverness; for otherwise we would discover how impoverished and down at the heels we are. Knowledge does not enrich us; it removes us more and more from the mythic world in which we were once at home by right of birth.

As I feel again the power of those words, I reflect on you and me and our modern culture. I recall my own drive to accomplish things in life, and I remember the hundreds of clients and students I have spoken with who have come to a place in their own lives where the quest for prestige and status, fancy cars, and financial security has left them empty and lonely. We were trained to seek answers to our inner poverty in the outer world, in status and external success. But it is an *inner achievement* we require, not an outer one. We need to heal that deep loneliness of spirit we inherit from a culture that is too clever and not enough wise. We need to *heal our rifts with God*.

As a poor child, I did not know I was poor until I got older and visited my wealthier friends. It's an old story: We can't see ourselves clearly until we get the perspective of others' lives. Similarly, I wasn't able to see my spiritual poverty until my early thirties, when I was thrown into a sink-or-swim breakdown of the world as I knew it. I wasn't able to see it before that time because everyone I knew or saw had a rift as deep or deeper than my own.

When I began to recover from my own spiritual poverty, it became easily visible everywhere in our society. We are starving. We are suffering, and most of us can't see the terrible shape we're in because everyone around us is suffering from the same malady. Like the cows that unknowingly trampled their life-giving spring, we blindly despoil our spiritual heritage. But there is no wise farmer around to remedy the situation. Instead, our leaders in government, education, entertainment, religion, and the media, who are entrusted with the farmer's job, are even more spiritually wounded and blind than the rest of us. No wonder Mother Teresa was aghast at our unrecognized plague.

My Own Spiritual Recovery

The first step in recovery from anything is awareness, and that awareness often comes during a journey. As we learn from mythology, the hero's journey is about this kind of awakening, of seeing oneself in perspective. I was thirty-two when I embarked on my own mythical journey into the mountains of Utah from my adopted home in Southern California.

Frankly, it was a journey within a journey. That's what made it feel so hopeless for me in the beginning. I had thought that leaving my childhood home in Ohio for California only thirty months before was the journey of my life. It had changed me so profoundly that I knew I could never go home again. Yet here I was on the road once more, trying to find I knew not what by leaving my adopted home in Los Angeles. I have heard it said that creatures in pain keep moving from one locale to another in a subconscious maneuver to escape that pain. The Twelve Step groups call it "doing a geographical." I was discovering a real talent for it.

I was a creature in pain who kept moving. I left the Los Angeles area in much pain and confusion, hoping to find my way in life, the reason I had moved to L.A. two and one-half years earlier. Two long-term dreams had failed during my stay there, and I felt the weight of those failures. First, my seven-year marriage, long on the rocks, had finally turned belly-up and refused to revive. It was a merciful death for both of us, I knew, but something that wasn't supposed to happen to Ohio farm boys. And second, I had finally been forced to admit I was not cut out to be a college writing and literature teacher or a publications writer. From the time I left factory work and started college on the GI Bill at age twenty-five, I had loved writing poetry, which offered as much hope of providing a living as a special talent at tiddlywinks. So my farmer's practicality told me that if I got a college teaching credential, I could write while I taught. Somehow, I had never considered that something as noble-sounding as college teaching could feel as meaningless to me as working in a factory had felt years earlier. Not all change gives us what we want.

It was not as if I had chosen my career blindly. Like most people, I chose carefully from among all options, following my practical reasoning, which was all I knew at the time. I loved literature, just as I loved my wife. I chose both because I had been looking for something—an answer to my pain, I suppose. I know now that I had always carried a great deal of pain. I had gone from the farm to the army during the Vietnam War years, and later I worked in an appliance factory. I was always looking for that elusive sense of happiness, and nothing seemed to help. When I met the woman who became my wife, I hoped that marriage would fill the void I couldn't fill on my own. At twenty-two, I felt that love and lots of sex, food, and alcohol could cure anything. But after three years I had to admit that I had to have more. *A creature in pain keeps moving.*

College was my next plan for redemption, of which my wife did not approve, even less when I discovered a love for literature. How did *that* make sense as a profitable career field? She was a practical woman, and despite my propensity to hard work born of farm upbringing, I was proving to be a very impractical man who would never be satisfied with only the "normal" things in life—the house, kids, and a station wagon. By the time we divorced six years later, she saw me as a failure at the important things in life, and a large part of me agreed as I drove into Ogden, Utah, my home base for my Utah sojourn. The old dreams were gone, and the farm boy within was still damned if he could figure out how poetry writing—my alleged reason for moving to Utah—would parlay into a crop worth counting on. But I felt I had no option but to try.

Illness and Unhappiness: Metaphors for the Rift

I didn't know it at the time, but I was spiritually sick when I arrived in Ogden, and I had been for a long time. Like most everyone in

America, I was raised a materialist. If things didn't work out with one place or in one job or relationship, I didn't look within to find the problem: I naturally assumed it lay with the place, the job, or the other person. Therefore, I had kept moving. I had been unhappy with farm work, so I tried painting houses, then auto maintenance, then the army, then the factory and marriage, then college, and so on. I became a heavy drinker, a sex addict, an academic—but the pain continued. As the years went by, I developed a bad back, arthritis, a stomach problem, headaches from allergic reactions, and severe anxiety.

Only after my time in Ogden did I realize that all my illnesses and unhappinesses were but metaphors for my spiritual *dis-ease*. What was real was that I was cut off from my Self—and the stress of that most unnatural of separations manifested physically and emotionally. I now know that this process generated by loss of Self cannot help but happen. It is hard-wired into the system. "As above so below," said the ancient sages. "As within so without." Whatever is true in consciousness manifests in physical reality.

I had spent years running from my own inner demons, thinking they were external to myself. But now, as I drove into Ogden in my broken yellow Ford Pinto, I entered a sort of Twilight Zone of the soul, a setup by the universe. I was at the end of my rope, I had hit bottom. Battered senseless by my strivings, I gave up the ego ghost and let life unfold on its own. It has been said that salvation can be found in great danger. I was in the most profound danger a human can encounter. And as I was soon to discover, this very danger was also my salvation. I was engaged in a battle for my soul.

My first few weeks in Ogden were filled with utter and profound misery. I had let go into the void, and the void was dark and painful. Without a woman for the first time in a decade, I was thrown into a feeling of deep abandonment, which I now know to be my chief malady, from which I had always run like the wind. Now that the wind had stopped, all of my symptoms got substantially worse as the abandonment increased. The greater the pain, the more I drank to relieve it. I began to understand that even my love of women was on one level another attempt to shut off the pain of my own soul. But I did not understand for some time that only when I healed the source of this abandonment would the symptoms diminish or even disappear.

Recovering the Early Wounds

Despite my prodigious drinking to escape it, my soul began to stir and awaken. Having no woman at hand on whom to project my powerful emotions, I began to feel them deeply. I would meditate first thing in the morning after taking a short drive up into the mountains. Sitting by a rushing stream or the large reservoir in the upper valley, I would open myself to the water and to nature, surrendering to their force as I surrendered to my surging emotions. Poetry would spew from me in gushes, leaving me scrambling for pen and paper to record it. Great emotions would pour forth as I scribbled and sobbed, wracked by feelings long buried and still not understood. Although the process of writing it was morbid and full of pain, the poetry allowed me to tap the deep springs of my soul in a way I had never before experienced. I would not have called it *spiritual* at the time. I called it *passionate verse*. Only time would allow me to understand that such passionate verse is by its very nature spiritual.

I would often continue writing poetry after I began drinking in the afternoon and evenings. (I was never a morning drinker and had no desire even then to drink before late afternoon.) With alcohol to lubricate my emotional and symbolic joints, the poetry and tears would flow even stronger, often taking me into a painful ecstasy I had never before experienced. As one with a lifelong habit of avoiding and denying my painful emotions, I was beginning to appreciate their transmuting and transcendental power. I also began to appreciate the healthful relief that feeling and expressing emotions and other shadow material bring to the body/mind.

Another tool I developed at that time was "daily scripting," a way of stabilizing identity. I say *developed* with a smile, because nothing I did for myself then was thought out and logically discovered. I was a desperate and anguished man, fighting for survival. My ego identity—my worldview, my roles, everything I knew to be true—was dissolving, and nothing had arisen to replace it. Often, when out walking or driving, I would experience panic attacks and would have to stop for a while to regain my composure. For sheer survival, I developed a centering technique I call "waiting out the devil," which I teach even now to anxious people: it entails simply allowing the emotions to be, without resistance. I developed daily scripting to help me deal with that same feeling of disintegration and panic.

I got in the habit of writing down, scripting, what I *knew* to be true first thing in the morning, right after my dream work: "Who am I? Where am I? What am I doing and where am I going?" That is the sort of thing I would ask myself. Then, with my thoughts turned off as much as possible, I would rapidly and continuously answer myself for pages. Many mornings I could not start the day without this scripting, for it gave me a sense of my existence, a sense that I at least knew something about myself and what was happening to me. It relieved the fear, and since I did not yet know how to use fear for transformation, I was grateful for that relief.

My dreams finally helped me understand what I was trying to say with my poetry and scripting. The symbolic language of dreams is not different from that of poetry, drama, or myth. All arise from the depths of human consciousness and have meaning for those with what Christ termed "eyes to see and ears to hear." And almost all my early dreams were set on the farm where I was born and reared. I recall dream after dream of cleaning excrement out from under the floorboards of the old farmhouse. Gradually, I began to understand that it was simply my unconscious agenda for the moment: uncovering what had been so long repressed and digging it out. I was doing that with my poetry, my uncontrolled emotions, and my dreams.

These experiences were simply cleaning out the stream—shoveling out the cow dung and debris that blocked the Source of Life from flowing. After a time, I began to understand that fully. I remembered my last few months of the L.A. days, when I would get drunk and curse the sky for my misery, begging for something to live for, something to pull me from my bed in the morning with a passion for life. I wanted that more than anything, an all-consuming passion that would make me whole. Here in Utah, my dreams began to make sense to me. I felt they were telling me that the passion for life would flow when my inner spring was cleared of its ancient debris.

I found that a huge rock blocked the stream. Its name was "Suicide." When I was six years old, my father committed suicide, leaving my mother and five children, of which I was the youngest. It was a terrible time for all of us, financially and emotionally. Since his insurance was invalidated by the suicide and there was no will, the farm went into probate and we had to sell most of our valuable assets to retain the property. We were instantly thrown into poverty. By far the most damaging effect of all, however, was emotional.

My family rolled a stone into the spring of emotions when Dad died. No one spoke of it. Mother chose not to cry, "to protect the children," she said. And the children followed suit, pretending everything was all right to protect Mom. We all did the best we could at the time. I, at six years of age, did not understand death, but I felt the sudden shutdown of emotions, which I experienced as personal rejection. In my primitive child's reasoning, I could not imagine why else people would withdraw from me, pull away and avoid intimacy, unless I were personally repugnant.

I felt abandoned and rejected by my father, of course, and I felt guilty and ashamed. If he left, it must be because I was a bad boy, because I was not good enough. The family's sudden withdrawal confirmed my feelings. Something was wrong with me. I was not worthwhile. I felt unloved and unlovable and very nervous and anxious. After all, being the miserable wretch I was, what would prevent the rest of them from leaving?

I developed a new strategy for survival at that time which would cut me off from my spiritual source for over twenty-five years. Based on this new belief that I was an unworthy and unlovable wretch, I adapted a pattern of taking responsibility for others' emotional needs, particularly my mother's, by becoming the strong "little man" upon whom she could always lean. Note the importance of this new stance: unconsciously, I had drawn the conclusion that since I was unworthy and unlovable, I must earn the love that I now know God offers freely. I had unwittingly created a rift with God that would keep me scrambling for survival in an unfriendly universe for decades to come.

Suicide had always been a distinct possibility for me, once I was old enough to understand and defend it. Father had done it, I reasoned. Father was a good man. If he did it, he must have had a good reason. If his suicide was justifiable, then so was my own. At times, I was obsessed with taking my own life. Suicide was my way out if all else failed, and I would not let go of its possibility. I thought of it as a way out during my three army years, when the factory and marriage scheme didn't work, during my college years, and especially when my first marriage fell apart in Southern California. During these first months in Ogden, when I faced my pain as never before, death was my constant companion, the subject of my dreams, and the central character of my poetry. As time wore on, I became more and more aware that this was a struggle for life or death. Life had so far proved a dead end for me. I could be successful in it, in worldly terms, but not happy. I could not go back to that wasteland of a life without meaning and passion. Unless I could come to terms with my demons and find a meaning in the madness of life, I had no reason to go on with it. I was enjoined in a true life-or-death struggle, with only my poetry, booze, dreams, nature, and a realization that I had no choice but to wrestle with my demons to sustain me.

As the Christmas season approached, my dreams and writings showed no sign of resolution. The theme of crap under the floorboards continued; anxieties and conflicts remained. The deep psychological conflicts didn't seem to be responding to the attention I was giving them. I still felt alone and alienated. Divorced without possibility of reconciliation from the rational-material view of life—with its high promises of material achievement, degrees, status, and competition—I had found nothing to replace it. I had no mythos, no reason for being to organize my life and give it direction and structure.

Saved by the Light on Christmas Day

I must confess that I have hesitated to write about this next episode, in spite of it being the turning point of my life. Part of my hesitation is an egocentric fear of ridicule, a fear that people will see me as foolish.

But the other part of this hesitation is genuine concern that others in crisis not be led to believe that they must have such a dramatic divine intervention to heal their own rifts with God. It's simply not true, and it would be harmful to believe so. I must emphasize that I had no spiritual or even psychological assistance in Ogden except a half-dozen books written more for therapists than for neurotics fighting for their lives. I rather wish for simplicity's sake that I had worked out my problems entirely on my own without cosmic assistance, but I didn't. I believe the following episode came because there was no other help available to me.

At noon on Christmas Day, while I was playing at the frozen edge of my favorite lake with two children, I was struck by a ball of light. I was nearest to the boy, who felt its force and ducked with me. His mother observed it from the car, parked nearby, and ran to my aid. I was stunned. I had not seen it coming, and I could only imagine that I saw it streak back into the sky afterward.

We didn't know what had happened. We did not think of the biblical account of Paul's being struck by the light, nor did we know that such events—when men and women were hit or somehow influenced by a powerful light that changed their lives—have happened periodically throughout recorded history. We were simply frightened and left for home immediately. The woman and I noted the oddity that this strange event had occurred on Christmas Day while I was by the lake with two children, whom I consider my adopted kids. And then we forgot about the experience as soon as possible and went on with the holiday festivities. Its implications were too unsettling to people as skeptical as we about the mystical aspects of life.

I was well schooled in repression and denial. As soon as the incident was over, I dismissed it. Only years later, when I read studies and personal accounts of others who shared this experience of light, did I begin to understand its significance. The change in my Ogden life after that was remarkable, however. My "clearing out the spring" suddenly took on a mystical dimension. Certainly the pain and torment continued: the conflictual dreams, the occasional cleaning out of manure, the poetry and crying. But now they had a spiritual aura about them.

I began to have what I called "cosmic dreams": Riding whales over first the ocean and then the land, all the while singing—I still recall the melody—"Life is but a shadow: it just keeps on going." Visiting a saint in a temple, where I was told the Truth about existence. Each night brought new dreams of transcendence, and each day brought transcendental experiences in nature and in my poetry.

I began to hear a long chanting hum by the lake in the mountains and to experience spontaneous past-life episodes, which I still do not understand and hesitate to discuss. Once, while driving back down through the pass, I *became* an Indian warrior on a pinto horse and almost wrecked before I could curb the car and regain my ordinary awareness. Life was suddenly very different from ever before. Thank God I had the books by Carl Jung—whose works validated my experiences as mystical and transformational rather than psychotic—to read during this period, or I might have had myself committed.

One particular dream gave my life new direction and meaning and prepared the way for my own personal myth. I was by now a follower of Jung's "synchronicity," which validated the mystical experiences I was having daily as "meaningful coincidence." This dream bridged the gap between the suddenly mystical world I was now experiencing and the practical world to which I would soon return.

I awoke in the middle of the night with a picture of a Joshua tree (that distorted bush found in the Southern California desert) in my mind. It was accompanied by the word *Joshua* and a wide-awake compulsion to find out what it all meant. Without hesitation, I arose from my bed, searched out my dog-eared college edition of the Bible, and found the book of Joshua. Every word I read was illuminating. I understood it not only in the literal sense but also symbolically. And every word applied directly to my life. It became at that moment a plan for my life, a blueprint, an answer to modern man's soullessness. I read for the remainder of the night, and every word became a part of my *waking dream*.

The Hebrews, you recall, were stranded on the banks of the river Jordan. Moses, their leader from the days of bondage in Egypt through forty years of wandering in the desert, had proved unworthy to cross because he had struck his staff on a rock in anger. His was the "old con-sciousness," which was unworthy to cross into the Hebrew Promised Land. His people had to wait till his death—which I knew to be the old way of unsurrendered thinking—before they could cross to the "promised land" of God-surrendered consciousness. Joshua, whose spoken name awoke me that night, was the "new man," reared from youth in the new awareness of God's magnanimity to those who sur-rendered to Him.

Joshua led his people into the Promised Land, where they fought the enemy and met with much success until they reached Jericho, where they experienced defeat. The "new man," Joshua, asked God why His promise of victory had been broken and was told that one among Joshua's men had held back some gold, all of which had been promised to God. Once the gold was surrendered to God, Joshua had only to lift his arm (thus, the Joshua tree), the walls of Jericho fell, and the city was theirs.

From that moment forth, I have had my own personal myth, and my life has had a deep and profound meaning that it never had before. Moses, to me, was that old state of mind, which certainly had freed me from slavery to my childhood myths and brought me to California and then Utah, but which was still mired in an unsurrendered state of con-sciousness that continued to be run by the ego and its neurotic view of the world. Life was still an angry and difficult place for a Moses man who would petulantly strike his sacred staff on a rock if he didn't get his way.

Joshua, on the other hand, was totally surrendered. No fits of anger at God for him. When things didn't go his way, instead of pouting and ranting, he asked God to clarify the matter: "Hey," he might have said. "I know *You* make good on your promises. What have *we* done to screw things up?" Joshua was the model of one who lived in God conscious-ness and let his life unfold moment by moment in the perfect faith that God's will for him was the right will and that there was no other way to live but by God's grace and will. Joshua was a man who had healed his rift with God.

From the moment I read the book of Joshua in that illumined state, I knew that his way was my way. Running my life from the ego had proved disastrous. I could not live fully without knowledge of the grace of God. At that moment on that day, I decided to never again base my life on the ego's logic and rationale. My job was to learn how to discern spiritual knowledge from mere rational knowledge and to follow the path of God. I had no choice, you see. To not do so was to continue the folly of the past. Somehow inside of me was a sense of the infinite, universal intelligence, which I could apprehend through bodily senses, dreams, emotions, poetry, the higher logic of scripting and creativity, and in the arms of nature. This was the water of life that flowed through my being, my inner spring. Egocentric life, I realized, is but a weak and inflexible reasoner, a cow who despoils the spring that gives it life.

This was the turning point when my rift with God began to heal. No longer feeling unworthy of God's love, I lived *for* God. Although my psychological issues continued to move toward resolution, they now had a container in which to cook to completion, which continues to this day. I began to live and thrive while learning to further heal them. When I drove out of Utah a few months later, I knew that only one thing had meaning for me: to become more aware of my soul and its destiny in life and to help others find the same "promised land" within themselves.

All of my life since, twenty-one exciting years, has been nearly an automatic journey, a carrying out and refining of the sense of wonder I experienced during my Ogden sojourn. I left Utah a fully surrendered man, and gradually I found my way to the San Francisco Bay area, drawn by nothing more than a sense that this is the "right" place to carry out my destiny and life, which I have never again yearned to terminate. Within weeks after arriving, through a number of miraculous events, I began the work of helping people heal themselves. With this newly won sense of God consciousness, everything I do is guided and meaningful. Without it, I'm certain my life would have continued to be the wounded mess it was before my awakening. I knew then that I and most people lived what has been called "lives of quiet desperation." But today I am just as certain that if these people could see the possibilities I began to see during those months in Utah, they would begin the journey to inner healing. That was my only plan as I left Utah—to help people learn what I had learned.

Discovering the Holistic Health Connection to the Rift

At the time I came back from Utah and began working with people, I had no ideas about getting involved with holistic health. I knew only that I had been in great physical, emotional, and mental pain and now I was much relieved. I had found my Self and God, had recovered my soul in some way, and wanted to help people do the same. But I also remembered that I had not turned within simply because someone told me to; I turned within because *there was no place else to go*. I suffered enough physical and emotional pain to knock me to my knees for a while. Only when all other means known to me had failed had I opened myself to other possibilities. *And only when we open ourselves to new possibilities can the healing begin.*

I was drawn to practice in the holistic health field because of my new awareness that everything in heaven and earth is interconnected. Through my own experiences, I could see the complementary role that physical and emotional suffering may have in spiritual awakening as well as the healing role that spiritual growth may play in overall health. It was a time when the holistic shift was beginning to happen. But most people still relied on the modern medical paradigm for everything having to do with health. Today, most of us have come to understand that modern medicine is but a scientific-material answer to material problems, wondrously effective in its own right but insufficient for the full mystery of human health and wholeness.

The majority of modern medical practitioners and their patients continue to operate on the biomechanical model of health. It remains the most effective system for repairing certain mind/body problems. When some part of the human mechanism breaks down, they give little thought to the whole. They simply try to fix it, and they forget about the rest. This approach works much of the time, even in psychology, wherein labor the so-called "doctors of the soul." And as long as it works, they will continue to use this paradigm to fix ailments and pain, pretty much as they fix their cars. Who can blame them for continuing to use a system that works in these matters? We can thank our good fortune that such a system exists when we need it.

People look outside the scientific-material paradigm to alternative therapies because they instinctively know that *fixing is not healing*—and because they are becoming aware of the shockingly high rate of iatrogenic (caused by medical intervention) illnesses and death. I have found a much greater willingness in these people to look within for the answers they have not found in hospitals and on couches, a willingness to look at their jobs, their relationships, and their own inner wounds in order to heal themselves.

It is no accident that, in this age of personal experience and inner authority, spirituality and healing go hand in hand. Many of the same people who visit holistic healers, where they are treated as individuals in charge of their *own* healing and encouraged to get in touch with their own inner healing resources, flock to experiential churches and spiritual groups, where they are encouraged to engage their *own* personal relationship with God. This is a societal movement emphasizing *personal experience* rather than the outward authority of dogma. The *healer* is within the individual: *God* is within each individual. State-authorized healers and gods are replaced by the individual's inner experience and guidance.

When I experienced my Self and God for the first time in Utah, there were no metaphysical or self-health bookstores in the area. Upon moving to the San Francisco Bay area, again I found very few. The new consciousness I'm speaking about had begun but had not yet flourished. Hypnotists were looked upon with suspicion by the general public. Acupuncture, herbalism, and out-of-mainstream spirituality were still on the fringes, scorned and derided by institutionalized medicine and religion. Times have rapidly changed. In the years since, a vast wave of holism has flooded upon us, transforming the way people heal and relate to God.

I have watched with great interest as scientific research begins to document this profound transformation. One study, for example, shows that one-third of Americans seek unconventional healthcare:

425 million visits to alternative therapists compared to 388 million visits to Western medical folks. And since insurance companies are invested in the Western medical model, most of the $13.7 million that people spent on holistic and alternative sources came out of their own pockets. Amazingly, even when conventional therapies are free and alternatives cost money, people choose the alternative route, often against the advice of medical doctors. While we once treated doctors as all-knowing gods not to be questioned, we are now thinking for ourselves and consulting our own inner wisdom about what is good for us.

Another interesting study, by Lisa Berkman of Yale Medical School, shows how important something as unscientific as *love* is to healing. Her study of two hundred older men and women with heart attacks showed that people who are alone die at *three times* the rate of those with friends to help them. A full 53 percent of those with no close personal support died within six months, compared with 36 percent with one person and 23 percent with at least two friends available. Love, the scientists figure, alters the brain chemicals believed to lower blood pressure and stress response. That is the biochemical explanation. Holistic folks know simply that when we leave love and spirit out of our healing, we don't heal.

Perhaps a part of the benefit of having family and friends around—love—is that we have someone with whom to share our inner feelings and emotions. Professor Hans Eysenck of London University presented data kept on people in Germany and Yugoslavia since the 1960s showing that "people who bottled up their emotions under stress were likely to be more prone to cancer while angry and aggressive types ran more risk of heart disease." Eysenck reported that even smoking is less harmful than a negative reaction to stress and that helping people to express their emotions in a healthy way through counseling is very helpful to their health. Healing the rift with Self is obviously important to health.

I have found several studies that show a direct connection between religion and health. Some show that simply belonging to a strongly religious organization such as the Mormon or Seventh-day Adventist churches brings about greater overall health. Dr. Thomas Oxman of

Dartmouth Medical School, reporting on a study in the *Journal of Psychosomatic Medicine* of 232 people after heart surgery, says that religious faith and social connections "give people a sense of comfort and belonging and a more positive mood," which affects our autonomic nervous system for better health.

Other studies, however, point out that just going to church without getting anything out of it won't lend the full health benefits. A specific study of older folks on Hawaii's Kauai by Dr. Robert Schmidt at California Pacific Medical Center in San Francisco found that spirituality, "a belief in a higher power, not necessarily religiousness—was possibly the most important key to long life." When I read this study, I remembered the clear, happy eyes of a ninety-year-old woman I met during my days of researching spiritual approaches. The spirit I felt when she looked at me inspires me still. As I looked at her smooth forehead and felt her radiant energy, I knew she was healthy because she had no reason not to be. After years of struggle to overcome an early childhood spiritual wound and its physical manifestation as arthritis, she had finally made peace with her pain and with God. So often they are the same wound. Having healed her rift with God, she could rest in the pure knowledge that she was one with the infinite and had nothing to fear.

Finding and Refining My Work

It was in the course of helping people that I learned and developed many of the skills and perspectives which I use today: relaxation techniques, imagery, bodywork, acupressure, process work, dream work, creative expression, and meditation—all tools that I also use to keep my own inner spring clear and nourishing. And I discovered the sacred spring of yoga, a method of both holistic healing and spiritual enlightenment that is thousands of years old. These practices helped me to become clear and healthy and helped me to notice how deep and pervasive the rift with God was in the people I was helping as well as how various were its manifestations.

I noticed, for example, how many people abhorred the word *God*, acting offended if they heard it, but would then go on to say that they believed in a "higher power" of some sort. Others firmly believed in a God but were vehemently opposed to all forms of organized religion. Still others were so steeped in rational materialism that they considered even the mention of a greater power a slide back into the "dark tide of mysticism."

In exploring other people's pain as I had explored my own, I was shocked to discover how often their greatest wounds were caused by schools and churches—from church schools with vicious nuns and seducing ministers to atheistic science teachers and overzealous parents. I discovered that they often rejected God because of these hurts, completely damming up their connection to the waters of life to avoid the pain and the risk of being open to further abuse. Who could blame them for shutting down to protect themselves? It seemed their only defense. Yet that defense caused them to suffer a fate which I have found to be worse than death—a meaningless and pain-filled life.

It was only later that I began to understand what Jung, Mother Teresa, and many other enlightened teachers have understood about our world: modern society itself is wounded and cut off from God, its source, and most of us, because we were raised by wounded members of that society, have inherited that wound from them and are in dire need of healing our rift with God. This need is not a trivial thing affecting only one area of our lives. It is our greatest need, encompassing *every aspect of our lives*, and it is at the root of many of our physical, emotional, and societal ailments.

After healing much of my rift in Utah, I discovered that most of my physical and emotional ailments were either healed or greatly improved. I realized then that my soul wounds were intricately connected with my physical and emotional health, and I have observed the same to be true for many of the people I have taught and counseled over the years. Over time, I have come to understand how important it is to reach a broader audience with this message, to participate in the healing of the larger society, for the soul wounds we experience happen in the context of our society, which is itself wounded. *A wounded society, cut off from its spiritual foundation, cannot help but produce an abundance of wounded individuals. These people may then risk even more wounding if they turn for help to professionals whose own wounds remain unrecognized and thus unhealed.*

In the pages that follow, I present a few of the insights, anecdotes, ideas, and inspirations from over twenty years of teaching and private practice. I have found that we learn not so much by rational discourse as through experience: "I read and I forget; I see and I remember; I do and I know," says the old Chinese proverb. Stories of how others have dealt with challenges similar to our own are the closest thing to actual experience a book can offer, especially when we are also talked through the journey step-by-step. I was raised on this method of communicating ideas as a child on the farm. It is as familiar to me as the handle on an old hoe.

Whenever possible, I've tried to adhere to this more immediate method of communication, recognizing that it appeals to both our rational and our mythological learning abilities and has the potential of uncovering that long-hidden spring at the center of our beings. As I found in Utah, that spring can be discovered when we explore the rift, the pain and suffering that has long kept us from our birthright of peace and love. My desire is that you, the reader, recognize within these pages your own rift with God and get on with the journey of finding that God-spring within that heals all wounds.

— 1 —

SEEING BEYOND SYMPTOMS
TO THE SOURCE

WHEN HE FIRST WALKED through my door, Bob looked like the G.Q. model of success, from his Brooks' Brothers suit to the confident smile on his face. He was an outgoing and charismatic man, his dark hair swept back from his handsome face as if by a hairdresser not five minutes earlier. Truthfully, I felt intimidated. This was obviously a powerful and successful man. What could he possibly need from me, at the time a rather inexperienced holistic consultant specializing in habit control?

For all his outward perfection, Bob was a humble man. Within minutes I felt as if I had known him all my life. I genuinely liked him, though something about him struck a discordant note deep inside me, causing me to squirm, the way I do when a person I meet reminds me of something in myself I don't quite recognize or care to admit. Even before he told me why he had come, I knew that helping him was very important to me—for far more reasons than either of us were able to admit at the moment.

It turned out that Bob was concerned about his drinking problem, which he designated at first as "slight" but which grew worse as the conversation continued. In fact, he finally admitted, he was still drinking after years of trying every expensive and inexpensive cure of his time. He had been to a psychiatrist and had taken Anabuse, the "chemical cure," which had made him miserably sick when he drank—until he quit taking it six weeks later. He had spent months in expensive treatment programs, only to begin drinking soon after he walked out the door. He had attended hundreds of Alcoholics Anonymous meetings— the self-help program which proved to the world that peer-support groups work—which only seemed to make him drink more than ever. As I watched his face and body transform from an erect and smiling mogul to a slumped and desperate man, I found myself embarrassed and shy, as if I had accidentally opened the wrong door and walked in on someone disrobed and performing some obscene and humiliating act. I found myself wanting to close that door, and for both of us to pretend it had never opened.

I imagined that my reaction to him was part of Bob's burden. I didn't like seeing his dark side any more than he wanted to disclose it. This collusion of deceit makes it difficult for us to reveal the seamier side of ourselves. We all want to believe in the self-image we allow the world to see; none of us wants to expose or be exposed as the miserable creature who now sat before me. Yet at certain points in all our lives we are forced to acknowledge just such creatures within us. And those who witness this acknowledgment don't want to because it reminds us of our own dark shadow. We prefer to search for heroes and avoid drunks.

Bob's life was in the kind of shambles only another addict would understand. The founder of a successful Silicon Valley computer technology firm, he was an amazingly astute businessman of much wealth. But his business was falling apart at its fiscal seams. He had lost the confidence of his associates and was in danger of losing the company. His wife of fifteen years still loved him deeply but had left him six months earlier, having finally given up on his ever-pending recovery. His doctor told him that he had already sustained much liver damage and would not live past forty-five if he continued drinking. At forty-two and in the prime of his life, Bob was sitting—and drinking—on the edge of disaster.

"I'll be honest with you, Paul," he said, leaning toward me, elbows resting on his knees. "I've tried everything society has to offer people like me. As far as I'm concerned, you're my last chance. If you can't help me, I'm not trying anything else."

I felt both honored and terrified by his statement. My heart swelled with the honor that comes with being entrusted with sacred human hope, and it shuddered with the realization that he was so accustomed to failure at this appointed task that he could give up at any moment. I knew that my job—as his designated "last chance"—was to see what everyone else had missed. But would he stay around long enough for me to do my work? It was becoming very important to me that I not be the proverbial "last straw" placed on the back of his campaign for salvation.

But despite his seemingly precarious situation, Bob was one of the most motivated people I have ever met. Never successful at stopping drinking, he could never be accused of not trying. He was a binge drinker. He would quit for days at a time, swearing that this time he had it licked. Then, like a time clock, the instant would come for him to drink, and he could not help himself.

"Here I am, doing it by the books, everything the programs have told me to do, and boom, I'm gone. That deep yearning arises in my body like forty thousand pounds of pressure pushing outwards, and I need a drink." He paused, as if searching for a way to express the feeling, and when unable to find it, he waved his arms and raised his voice. "I need a *drink!* I feel at that time it's either shoot myself or take a drink, and I drink to save my life. Then I keep on drinking until I black out and wake up a week later in jail or in hell—usually both. My body is sick, my mind is gone, and I feel like death itself. I stay in bed for a couple of days, sure I'll never touch that crap again. After that, I'm normal for a few weeks, a real model citizen, until—like a coiled snake you can't see in the underbrush—it strikes again."

I understood Bob completely. I had been there. Since he had tried everything else—all the standard treatments—my job was simple. There was nothing else to do but look at that "coiled snake," the feeling that he would die if he didn't take a drink. I wanted to know all about that. I wanted immediately to ask him more. But did I dare be so bold in this first visit? The disparity between his perfect *G.Q.* image at the beginning of our visit and the desperate man he had now revealed was enormous. Might I not push him over an edge and scare him off if I asked him to imagine that feeling now? Perhaps it was too much too soon. On the other hand, I thought, if I show him no more insight than he has been getting elsewhere, might he not give up in frustration, feeling he has already been down this route? Finally I felt the answer in my body: we had to go for it.

"Bob," I said gently, "would you be willing to feel that 'coiled snake' you spoke of in your body right this minute?"

"But I don't feel it right now," he said. "I won't for at least a couple more weeks."

"That's OK," I assured him. "I know by the way you grimaced and held your stomach a while ago that you remember how it feels. It's good that it's not as strong as at those intense times, so we can work with it. Just close your eyes and let your body recall it as clearly as possible. It's important to face our demons, but on our own terms, with support, while we are strong and fully present."

"OK," he said, after a minute or two, eyes closed and intensely concentrating. "I'm scared as hell, but I can feel it. I can feel the snake, and I feel like running out of here and getting drunk right now," he said.

"Good. I'm right beside you, and I want you to remember that this isn't one of those bad times when you're all alone. We can make these feelings go away anytime we want. You and I just conjured them up a minute ago, and we can unconjure them. Remember that. And now, I want you to relax and ask your body what that feeling reminds you of. How far back can you trace these feelings?"

"Well, this is strange as hell," he whispered, after a short pause. "The second you said that, I felt like I'm back in seventh grade! What was I, thirteen? I was an altar boy in the church, and after mass, Father O'Leary asked me if anything was wrong. I was looking troubled, he said." Bob paused for a moment, contemplating the experience. "So I told him about Mom and Dad, how they were drunk every night and how Mom pushed me around, making me help her all the time, never letting me run around with my friends.

"Hell, that was the day she started hitting me in the head—slapping me. I told Father O'Leary because he asked, and I figured *nobody* should get away with that. She just kept at it, over and over, till I went nuts. I couldn't take it anymore, so I pushed her. She fell down on the floor and I ran out. That's right . . . I haven't thought of that in thirty years."

He paused, experiencing his feelings in this ancient memory for a few moments. I could almost hear the walls around that painful experience of the past crumbling and falling as he updated his emotional files. The memory had not been unconscious to Bob, even though he hadn't thought of it for thirty years. But the intensity of the emotion and its importance in twisting his life had never been recognized until that moment.

Because we are unable to deal with them at the time, our most traumatic emotional experiences are often shunted into our mental closet when we are young. This is the mind's defense mechanism for coping with the uncopable. Trapped there like radioactive waste in unstable containers, they quietly exude their poisons into our lives, shaping our relationships with ourselves and others—and with God. Finally, sitting on my couch nearly thirty years later, Bob was absorbing those feelings into his present life and dealing with them as an adult.

"It got worse after I talked to Father O'Leary," Bob said. "I wasn't going to tell him, but he asked. And I figured I had nowhere else to go. I mean, I loved the guy. I thought he was God, kind and omniscient and all. So when he asked, I felt relieved, like there really was someplace to go, someone to turn to. So I told him.

"He just kind of turns his back on me," Bob said in a choked voice which sounded like that of a thirteen-year-old. I could tell he was fully regressed and really experiencing it all as the child. "I'm just a kid, crying to him about my pain, wanting to be held and taken care of like Christ would have done, but he turns on me," he sobbed. "Father's friends with Mom and Dad. They're big in the church. Dad's a successful lawyer and they give a lot of money. Father even comes over to dinner sometimes. He gets real cold and stern with me and says it's never OK to hit your mother and I should go straight home and apologize to her. 'Honor thy father and mother,' he says. He doesn't believe me when I say I was just defending myself. He's like God to me, and he doesn't believe me."

Bob cried for a few moments, big belly sobs that wracked his whole body, the kind that touch into deep waters and move mountains. I took a risk and moved over to hold him, and he cried in my arms like a baby—perhaps as he had wanted to do with Father O'Leary when he was thirteen years old. Later, he told me it was the first real cry he'd had since the incident. After a while, the sobbing stopped and his face grew bitter and hard, reflecting an ancient fury.

"Right then I knew I was alone in the world and there was no place to turn," he said. "That's never changed in all these years. I bought everything the church and my parents tried to sell me. I bought that it was my fault. I bought that I had failed God. But there was just too much pain in being a child of God, and if it was all of them against me, well to hell with them all. Damned if I would let them get to me again. I just shut down and went home and let Mom kick the crap out of me for telling Father O'Leary—he told her, you know. But I never cried. And I never gave an inch. But I quit being an altar boy after that, and I quit going to church. Father O'Leary never heard another one of my confessions, and I have never again taken the sacrament. I had believed in God so much before this happened, and I felt betrayed, absolutely betrayed. I hated God after that. Ever since."

I was amazed at the depth and clarity of Bob's insights. I would have been more than satisfied that day with but a tenth of what he remembered and realized. In fact, I had been looking for a good place to close for the day, fearing that he was flying too close to the sun before the wings of his awareness were stable. However, eyes closed but seeing clearly, he was not about to stop the rays of clear thoughts that were shining so bountifully from his long dark mental skies.

"I followed all the rules after that. Got good grades. Went to college and excelled in everything. But I also started drinking. Went on binges. When the pressure built up, I'd let off steam with booze. It seemed to work. I never lost my temper with Mom or anyone else from then on. Prided myself on my ability to control my temper. But the binges got worse as the years wore on, and here I am.

"Funny," he said, opening his eyes. "I'm pissed off. I never knew that. I'm really mad. I'm angry at God, and I have been ever since that day.

And here I thought all along I had just turned atheist because religion's not logical. Ain't that a pisser?"

The Walking Wounded

Bob was but one of many spiritually wounded people I encountered when I returned to California after my experiences in Utah. In the course of our time together, Bob discovered that—besides the addictive power alcohol had over him—his overwhelming "snake" was a lot easier to manage once he repeatedly returned to and resolved that original wound. He discovered that this wound was when God—in the form of, first, his parents, then, the church and Father O'Leary—abandoned and shamed him at the time of his greatest need. He expressed his anger over and over to me, and later, at my urging, to an objective priest, who, unlike O'Leary, completely understood and supported him. A deeply religious man at heart, Bob needed to reconcile with the church in which he was reared. He also needed this emotional purging, for Bob had long before thrown out God with the abusers. Like hundreds of others I have encountered in the years since, he had mistaken the church or a series of wounding events for God and had suffered a severe spiritual rift for nearly thirty years—a rift that nearly cost him his life and everything dear to him.

Every wounded person finds something to ease his or her pain temporarily, even though it never goes away completely, remaining in the psyche to wreak havoc with physical or emotional health. Bob chose the pernicious magic of alcohol to charm his poisonous "coiled snake" out of his system, nearly killing his soul as well as his body. But other people choose other poisons, such as addictive work, perfectionism, codependent relationships, isolation and withdrawal, compulsive thinking, compulsive exercise or activity, violence, and many others. Some of these poisons are socially acceptable—even admired. And others, like Bob's, are not. In many respects, all addictive behaviors *work*, because of their dual ability to shut off pain and turn on the good feelings, feelings that remind the addict of life in the Garden before the Fall.

Few spiritual wounds are as clear-cut and powerful as Bob's because of the way it sliced across all of the important areas of his young life, quickly and permanently destroying his trust in his family, his idol-priest, the church, and God. The way he dealt with it—assuming all blame and using his suppressed shame and anger as motivation to excel—kept twisting his coiled snake tighter and tighter until the only spirit reliable for good feelings was the kind that came in a bottle.

Later on, Bob told me how his drinking made life bearable for him: "I remember my first drink like it was yesterday," he said. "I was four-teen, and my parents were out of town. My friend Harry spent the night with me and picked the lock on their liquor cabinet. We drank half a quart of vodka and filled it up with water after we finished. I hated it at first. But after a few minutes I felt my body start loosen-ing up, and I got so relaxed, like I hadn't a care in the world. I felt good for the first time in months, like all was right with the world and I was on good terms with everything. It was a lot like I felt when I was an altar boy, before the incident. I always felt so holy and peaceful then, helping Father O'Leary with the mass, like God was there and I was part of God, being his arms and hands and heart for the people. I really believed then, Paul. The alcohol never helped me believe again, but it helped me *feel* all warm and relaxed like I did in the innocent days. I never felt whole again after the incident unless I was drunk."

I later realized that the reason I was so taken with Bob and the many like him who followed was because I was one of them. Like Bob, I had experienced a rift with God at a tender age and had turned to alcohol, among other things, to bear it. I also had been wracked with shame and guilt, and I became an anxious and unhappy striver, always in search of something to stop the pain and rekindle the good feelings.

I had only become aware of my own wounds and begun to heal them a few years before I met Bob. Like him when he came to me, I discovered that "all roads lead to Rome"—that all my symptoms related back to that original rift with God. When I arrived in Utah a few years earlier, I had been suffering from severe arthritis pain, back problems, and stifling headaches, all of which virtually disappeared when I began to resolve my rift with God. With that healing came a new relationship with myself and life, and the understanding that the only work which had any meaning for me, from that point on, was to help relieve the suffering of others. From the moment I personally experienced the full ecstasy of my immortal soul, I also knew that the basis of that suffering came from a deep spiritual wound prevalent in our society as a whole.

Jack's Magic Chariot

Jack's is the poignant story of a young man who prefers disability to a rift with God. I encountered him in a convalescent hospital where I was teaching. He was a young man in his early forties, confined to a wheelchair and able to move only his hands, with which he guided his electric wheelchair. I felt compassion for him, struck down by a stroke so young in life, but my own assumptions about the misery of convalescent hospitals were challenged by the sparkle in his eyes as I spoke to the class he was attending. So one day I asked him how it was that he seemed so happy and content, given his circumstances.

"I think you know that answer, Paul, or you wouldn't say what you do in class. But perhaps you don't realize how true your words are when you say that happiness is found within ourselves and not in external success," he said. Then he turned his "magic chariot," as he called his wheelchair, abruptly around and led me out into the building's tiny courtyard.

"Before my stroke, I was a highly paid executive in a fast-moving Silicon Valley firm. I was smart and motivated, a real go-getter. Nothing was going to stop me in my drive to the top. I had no time for family or friends. All I did was work. I never stopped to see what life was all about because I *knew* it was about who got to the top of the heap first. And I had all the things and status that money could buy— until the stroke hit me. It was an act of mercy if there ever was one.

"I couldn't be happier that it happened, Paul. Honest. If I had been living any life of my own before it happened, if I had stopped working long enough to run or play ball, I might not feel this way. But I was *nothing*. This place doesn't look like much, but I've got a window and this little courtyard, and I actually see and relate to the people I encounter here. I'm *alive*, don't you see, for the first time, instead of living in my head, fighting desperately to fill the hole in my heart with outward success. I'm more alive sitting here in my *magic chariot* watching the birds in this garden than I ever was as a high-roller.

"And, Mister," he said, gazing pointedly into my eyes, "there are millions out there just like I was—the walking wounded, who'll not rest till they get something like this to slow them down."

Jack was right. I wasn't surprised by what he said. Jack was in a wheelchair, supposedly suffering from a purely physical problem. Yet he clearly saw it as a spiritual wound that eventually *manifested* as physical. At his stage of development, he did not find it worthy to search for the whys and wherefores of it, and neither did I. What I found soon after beginning my work was that we cannot helpfully separate our ailments into neat little packages labeled "physical," "mental," "emotional," and "spiritual." People are natural beings, and like the natural world from which we spring, we are part of greater realities, systems that act and react within and between ourselves. What is an emotional or spiritual issue at one time becomes a physical one at another. Our inner ecology is no different from our external; when we deplete our spiritual ozone, our whole physical system will be affected.

As I taught and counseled, I found that the common sense in people agreed with me, that they knew something else was involved in whatever ailed them besides the presenting issues. Most of the time they were pleased to find someone who would help them look beneath the surface of their ills to the source. Very frequently we found the source was literally the *Source*, the source of all life including our own—the godhead itself. Even more often we found it to be in that direction, toward the inner life of the person rather than the external.

Victor Frankl demonstrated this most clearly in his work with Logotherapy. During his years in Nazi extermination camps during World War II, he found that the very *survival* of inmates depended not so much on the amount of food or medical treatment they received from the Nazis but on the state of their inner life. If they had a passionate enough reason to live, they tended to make it. If they did not, they were as good as dead.

Jack confessed that the source of his earlier blindness was a critical, rationalistic father whose harshness and pressure destroyed Jack's self-worth and left him with nothing but an intense drive to prove himself worthy through achievement and financial success. Wasn't that a "passionate reason for living," such as the one Frankl studied? Evidently not. Unlike Frankl's subjects, who were fighting for survival, Jack's passion was founded on a spiritual wound—a deep sense of unworthiness, self-anger, and a feeling of being separate from all that is good, worthy, and holy. After his incident and its forced inner reflection, he readjusted his skewed vision and reclaimed his inner harmony, which he deemed much more valuable than a misguided and obsessive success drive.

Beyond the "All Is Physical" Myth

Jack's situation, which seems so obviously physical, strikes to the heart of our fascination with the physical and material. Seldom has anyone entered my office for the first time with any idea that their physical ailments might originate somewhere beyond the physical body. Yet as soon as we scratch beneath the surface and the evidence asserts itself, they say, "But of course. How could I not see that before?"

Dorothy never thought of herself as someone who needed help with her life. She was a strong Midwestern woman from a small town in Nebraska, a place where people handled their problems and kept their mouths shut. Yet here she was seeing a counselor for stress-related colitis. A counselor, of all things! And even more surprising, she found herself answering my questions about whether she might know on some level the origins of her illness by saying that she sensed it was related to her estranged relationship with God, that she would be a lot healthier and happier if she could find a way to heal the sense of violation and betrayal she felt when the Catholic Church and her fellow parishioners shunned her after her recent divorce.

"I don't know why I'm saying this," she said, wide-eyed and flabbergasted, her round face a picture of innocence. "I've never even thought about this before. But when you ask so directly like that, I feel like some part of me has known the answer all along, and I think it's the truth: I feel like I've been banished to hell for something that wasn't my fault. God's the one that left *me*, not the other way around."

I immediately understood Dorothy's conundrum. She was raised on a farm, just as I was. Perhaps it has something to do with the hard work and tough life, but we farmers in general seem to me to be emotionally constipated. We seem to have the most difficult time recognizing our painful or angry emotions and expressing them. I call it our "nice disease." I have made myself sick being nice, and I recognize the tendency in others, ex-farmers or otherwise.

Nevertheless, before anything else could happen, Dorothy needed to know what she felt and to feel all of it—till it was finished. *E-motions* are like the word says—meant to be in motion. They are currents of energy that, if blocked because they are perceived as negative, can stagnate and contaminate positive emotions such as joy, faith, trust, and love. If left in that condition for a long time, they can begin to manifest as physical symptoms, as in Dorothy's case.

With expression, of course, came the "core understanding" that would release her from pain and help her begin the *new life*. After all, Dorothy's wound did not originate with her rejection by the church. the sad truth was that she had *never* enjoyed a personal relationship with God. She had spiritual feelings that could be stirred by church rituals, but that was not, as she was to realize, a mature relationship with God.

"I see now," she said toward the end of our work, "that my problem started a long time before my divorce. Fred was my daddy. The church was my daddy and mommy. My rift with God started when I was a little kid, feeling unloved and unworthy of love. I started a scheme to get that love by being a good girl and obeying all the 'good Catholic' rules. Then I'd get love and feel worthy. But all I got was a bunch of kids, a philandering husband who treated me like my father did, and a lot of self-righteousness. If I couldn't feel *good enough*, I'd try to feel *better* than everyone by following all the rules. Well, I lost it all. And I'm glad. I feel lucky to have finally *got the shit out* that my body was telling me about with colitis, so I can face reality. Now I know who God really is, and I finally have a real life instead of a fantasy—at fifty."

A Society in Search of Health, Self, and Wholeness

We have experienced the beginning of a revolution in healthcare and spirituality in the past twenty years, and I believe that the millions of people who find themselves exploring alternative healing therapies and spirituality are drawn by a single wisdom: the soul's cry for wholeness. Despite the fact that most leading voices in today's revolution in both healthcare and spiritual development are medical doctors, *the people themselves* led us to this place, following their own soul-call for healing and wholeness. As in all revolutions, the people grew dissatisfied with what they were getting. They felt, as I felt, an inner urge for integration and healing that mere symptom removal could not satisfy. The people demanded a revolution with their pocketbooks by seeking alternative spiritual approaches and seeing holistic practitioners— both of which brought them back to their bodies, souls, emotions, and nature—usually against the advice and without the knowledge of their doctors, psychologists, and clergymen.

Linda was just such a person. She was involved in one of those never-ending quests—weight loss—when she found her way to my office. Of medium height with short dark hair, she had a somewhat quizzical look on her face as she introduced herself. I experienced a feeling I sometimes do in these situations, a sense of *recognition* of a fellow traveler seeking her greater Self. But I never tell people about this sense of recognition unless they have the same experience and share it first. And sure enough, when I asked her why she had come to see me, she answered, "Well, I came to lose weight, but I don't think that's why I'm *really* here. The minute we met I realized that I don't know what I want from you, that it's probably something far greater than weight loss. But whatever it is, I know it *has* to happen. So let's get started."

Something in Linda's eyes and manner revealed her secret to me right away. Although a successful CEO, she demonstrated an intense need to please. She tried to anticipate my every request and kept glancing at her watch to avoid going overtime on our hour together. When we explored that *eager-to-please* feeling, she experienced herself as a child in a hospital, recovering all alone from a serious illness. She recalled the rejection and abandonment she felt when, day after day, no one came to visit her. And as is typical with children, she blamed herself for the abandonment: *Something must be wrong with me. I'm not good enough.*

With no shoulder to cry on and no one to turn to, Linda shut down awareness of her body and soul, where the pain and abandonment feelings were so intense. She had no conscious choice in the matter, since the system automatically dissociates from what it cannot bear. I began to feel in my own body the pain behind Linda's eager eyes and helpful manner. A fellow pleaser, I also felt my own hurt. How many of us feel that same pain? I wondered.

When Linda returned home from the hospital, she became very helpful, gradually assuming her troubled mother's job as caretaker for the family. Looking back, she could see that she took on that job to secure her own place in the family. "If they don't love me, at least they will need me," she seemed to decide at some point. She also began to eat a great deal more food than before her illness.

"I needed security, and I needed to stuff those emotions," she said. "That's clear to me now. I didn't feel secure in the family. I felt I had to *earn* security by taking care of everyone, by becoming indispensable. But as I became the mother to everyone, I dug my own painful hole deeper and deeper. Mothers are seen as being there for everyone else but having no needs of their own. No one was there for me, so I turned to food for solace and love. I was there for them; food was there for me. It helped me stuff those painful emotions. But I realize now that I was bargaining away my body and soul in the process."

In the end, Linda decided it was better to feel her pain than to lose her soul. Few of us like to feel pain, and it is part of our evolutionary survival instinct to cut it off at all costs, as a fox will chew off its foot to escape a trap. But when we cut off our pain, we sever our heads from our emotions, bodies, and souls. We create a rift with Self— and a rift with God. As Linda recovered her pain, she gradually recovered her Self and the power behind all healing—God. Has she become slim? That is at long last a choice she has the power to make. Who could ask for more?

The stories of Linda, Dorothy, Jack, and Bob all take us to the same answer when we explore the question of *Who needs healing?* Each of them suffered from some seemingly physical problem—obesity, colitis, a stroke, a drinking problem—for which they had each sought extensive assistance from the healthcare establishment. In the end, however, their issues were not what they seemed to be.

The past twenty years of helping people with their problems have led me time and again to an understanding that there's more to health and fulfillment than our simplistic, materialistically biased contemporary philosophies comprehend. Things do not happen randomly and without cause in our universe. When we are *dis-eased*, we can well be assured that it has something to do with us and is not only a random happening. On some level of our being, it *makes sense*. This does not mean, of course, that we *cause* our problems. It simply means that we all have something to learn about ourselves. And I can only wish for all of us, when the moment for help and healing arrives, that we may encounter someone willing to ask the basic questions that help us not only to fix the symptom but to heal the deepest wounds from which the symptom arose.

Over and over again in my years of healing work, when I have asked the question "What is this related to in your life?" I have received answers that have surprised me and guided me in helping those in pain to greater awareness, greater wholeness, and greater wellness. Occasionally, the answers seemed irrelevant. But most of the time those answers spoke to a need for healing a rift with God—the deepest and most comprehensive wound of all.

We spiritually wounded people have a deep need for spiritual connection, a longing for the manna of heaven, but we fell from grace when we threw away the sacred cup of spirit along with the bitter

wine of our wounds and the great pain caused by them. By rediscovering, feeling deeply, and expressing this pain, we can begin to heal
our rifts with God and restore our lives to integrity and harmony—
for when we heal our rifts with God, we simultaneously encounter
and heal ourselves.

~ 2 ~

A RIFT WITH SELF IS
A RIFT WITH GOD

LYNNE IS A WONDERFULLY OPEN-HEARTED student and an ardent medi-tator. Having begun to heal her rift with God some years ago, she has since been in a long process of learning to live the life of the spiri-tually healed and preparing to help others do the same. In her mid-thirties, she is strong and dedicated, now teaching meditation at the same local college where she originally studied with me. She has also been studying healing and acupressure, and she had been preparing to open her own acupressure office—when the symptoms struck.

Her right knee suddenly became lame. She could hardly walk, let alone keep up her hectic schedule of working her "straight" job in computer technology during the day while seeing clients at night. Her zest for making this transition from a nonfulfilling job to her right livelihood as a bodyworker diminished appreciably. And nothing seemed to help. Medical doctors had no answer. Physical therapy only aggravated her condition. And even acupuncture failed to resolve her problem. In fact, although everyone had an opinion, no one had the solution to Lynne's hurt knee.

We decided to use Process Acupressure, a mind/body/spirit tool developed by Dr. Aminah Raheem, to address her problem. Shortly after beginning the session, I asked Lynne's soul to guide us in discovering the deepest truth about the knee. What message might it have for us in helping her to heal? Within seconds, I noticed Lynne's right foot slowly turning inward, almost coyly, with the toes leading. Continuing to watch that movement for a moment or two, making sure I wasn't seeing things, I finally called Lynne's attention to it. She had not been conscious of the movement at all. I asked her to continue doing it while being aware of her feelings.

"I feel like a little girl when I do that," she said after a moment. I asked her how old she might be as this little girl. "I must be no more than five years old. I feel very shy, and it's my way of being cute for my father." She frowned and seemed about to cry. When I asked her why, she said, "I'm very afraid of Dad. He yells a lot and I don't know how to deal with him, so I just act cute and irresistible. Then he melts and I feel safe." She frowned again.

"This time is different, though. He's making us move across town so he'll be closer to his job, and I'm really mad at him. I want to tell him how hurt and angry I am about this, how unfair it is not to consider me and my feelings about leaving my safe neighborhood with all my friends and having to start over in what seems to me a hostile new environment. But I can't express my feelings to him. I'm too scared. All I can do is be cute. Be the coy little daughter and look sad till Daddy holds me." She paused, and then she nodded her head vigorously in the exaggerated rhythm of a child. "I'm sad because I can't stand up for myself," she said.

"It's the same deal now, as an adult trying to go out and do my own work," she said, when I asked her to access her adult, professional mind and see how her coyness with Dad related to her present sore knee. "My right knee is my father side of my body, down in my foundation. I'm trying to stand on my own and don't feel I can support myself. My head thinks I'm a grown woman, capable of going out from the 'father' company and doing my own work, but my foot is telling me that I'm still that little girl, cowed by her daddy and unable to stand up for herself." She paused for a moment, head cocked as if listening to an inner voice. "OK. I get it," she said abruptly, opening her eyes and gazing firmly into mine. "I guess I've got some work to do with that little girl before I go out and do my own work."

Lynne, of course, is an unusually aware person who knows that *a rift with Self is a rift with God*. She is also a spiritual heroine, a state that Emerson described in his essay "Heroism" as "obedience to a secret impulse of an individual's character." Determined to fulfill her inner nature, she will do whatever it takes to grow. Having realized that her knee problem was rooted in an immature attitude, she knew that her further spiritual progress—doing her right work—depended on reconciling her adult aspirations with her "daddy's girl" attitude. And being a spiritual heroine, she was grateful to her knee—and her soul—for pointing out her lack of congruity.

KOYAANISQATSI: WORLD OUT OF BALANCE

Lynne, a longtime seeker of inner harmony, found in her knee a symptom of inner imbalance. Eastern and Western traditional cultures, knowing that such conditions in individuals or societies are symptoms of dis-ease, had words to describe them. Chinese acupuncture, for example, denotes the imbalanced quality of life force in energy channels as "excessive" or "deficient." *Koyaanisqatsi* is an American Hopi Indian word describing a world out of balance—out of balance with one's Self and Life, or God. What we find is that they are one and the same thing. If one is out of touch with her Self, she is out of touch with God, and the little piece of the universe within her is also out of balance with everything else.

Spiritual masters throughout time have given us a similar message, such as what Christ told his disciples: "The kingdom of God is at hand." When we are out of balance with our inner kingdom, our entire universe is disordered. We are part of a consciousness that is at once us and greater than us. We are part of a vast mystery, an infinite intelligence that moves the planets round the stars and interacts with us in such a way as to offer meaning to what appears as madness to the purely rational mind. To be aware of God in our lives—since God is within us—we must be aware of more than our rational minds. We must *know* and *reclaim* our bodies, our emotions, and our very souls.

We pride ourselves on our vast intellect, but we are forced to admit that our thoughts alone cannot keep our bodies alive for even a minute. Everything within us marches to the rhythm of a drum of which we know very little, an intelligence that grew us from universal substance, cell by cell, to form a unique entity with a unique destiny. That intelligence—which we cannot and never will duplicate with our little brains—continues to perform miracles every second, keeping all our systems synchronized and in healthy harmony twenty-four hours a day, often with little cooperation from us. It replaces every cell in our bodies countless times in each lifetime, heals our wounds when we incur them, and gives us the wonder of love as well as the genius to create art, literature, and a technology beyond the dreams of earlier generations.

This mystery within us is often called the Self, which others call the soul, our natural self, God or Goddess, the universe, and so on. My own unconscious, in a dream, told me to follow "the great God Inman," a play on the words *in man*, which I understood only when recalling the dream later for my wife. Obviously a much greater intelligence than our ego identity, the soul is inseparable from not only our own inner ecosystem and that of all beings, but it is also inseparable from the collective body of our environment, our universe, and all of nature. It is at once our own unconscious Self and the collective unconscious, which all beings share.

This is the true body/mind/spirit intelligence that runs our lives from conception to death. When we say, "He was a born artist," or "She was always a doctor, even as a child," we know whereof we speak. On this inner level we are always becoming, and each of us is born with certain innate talents, abilities, and predispositions. When we are in tune with this inner flow of the soul, we can follow life rather than worry it to death, and we can allow ourselves to unfold on schedule.

But we humans are trained to be out of joint with ourselves. Fixated on the intellect—forgetting it is only one of our many faculties—we grow out of touch with our bodies, our emotions, and our souls. We identify with the one-dimensional ego self, concerned only with status, pleasure, and power, and we form a rift with our real Selves—

and thus a rift with God. We grow out of touch with our instincts, emotions, and intuition, and we no longer live life as it was intended. Caught in the ego's fever of worry and anxiety over our security and status, we lose track of life's meaning and purpose. We no longer hear the body's wisdom about where to live and how long to work at what. We form a rift with our Selves. Like pampered house dogs that carry their food dishes to our ego master, we hear the hounds of heaven bay but have forgotten how to hunt—or why.

Our earlier—and sometimes later—experiences create unbalancing wounds from which we seldom recover. We repress our wounds and forget how to feel, and we can no longer experience the inner ecstasy of God union or feel the inner urgings of spirit and nature. When we have grown insensitive to our bodies, using them only as workhorses to "get the job done," we cannot experience the spiritual path and follow where it leads us. We become stiff automatons that follow national trends, watch the evening news, and save money for the next high-tech toy we become convinced we can't live without. We live in our heads, far from both our instincts and our intuition. We are out of touch with ourselves and are therefore out of touch with God, our Higher Self.

While most traditional healing systems—and most certainly Chinese medicine and India's Ayurveda—acknowledge the Self as a holistic consciousness encompassing all aspects of the person, modern systems, until recently, have not. In the past few decades, however, as holistic thought and spirituality grow in influence, more and more people are echoing the words of famed psychologist Rollo May: "The battle for health must be won on the deeper level of *the integration of the self*." And as Lynne and many like her have found, the rift with God remains unhealed so long as the rift with Self remains.

Koyaanisqatsi: A Society That Promotes Disharmony and Soul Loss

The state of koyaanisqatsi is a condition that exists in society as well as in individuals, with each reinforcing the other. Psychologically, this state is called *dissociation*, meaning that the individual's central intelligence loses contact with one or more of its parts. Indigenous healers often refer to it as soul loss. World out of balance. A state in which the child cannot hear her mother's call.

Clyde comes to mind when I consider how we become so cut off from ourselves. Early in life, he was abused by both his father and mother, which led to a form of self-abuse in adulthood. He came to me for help with his depression after conventional therapy and drugs had failed. As we began our work, I was appalled to discover how embattled his life was. Arising at 5 A.M., he worked at a frantic pace until 10 P.M., every day of the week, pausing only to inject his system alternately with coffee, cigarettes, sugar, and alcohol. Craving love and companionship, he left little time for it, spending his few free hours alone watching television before falling asleep in his chair at one or two o'clock in the morning. Such behavior is defensible during wartime or imminent starvation, but like most of us, Clyde was under no such pressure.

Clyde, of course, could see nothing unhealthy about his schedule. It was the way he had lived for most of his fifty years—and the way his parents had lived before him. Many of our parents, children of the Depression and World War II, were the same. It was normal. When I told him that it amounted to abuse of his system, he protested: "This is just the way I live. I'm not willing to change it. No, I'm not happy with it, but I don't know another way. If I worked less, I'd feel worthless. And if I didn't keep full of caffeine and nicotine, I'd fall asleep on the job. I don't see any way out."

I understood Clyde very well. I was reared in the same manner, as was my father, who literally killed himself for those values. Like Clyde, Father didn't "see any way out." Like it or not, we are all forced to march to the drum of our own cultural and social mores, unless we somehow manage to hear the beat of a different drum that calls us to find and follow our own path. Until then, we continue a similar cycle of abuse that child abusers are known to follow: reared by abusers, they abuse their own children because *that's all they know.* Similarly, because we were trained in childhood to sacrifice our bodies, emotions, and spirit to the god of material acquisition and success, we train our children to march to the same drum. *That's all we know.*

Desensitization is our primary tool. Weaned on such aphorisms as "Waste not want not," "A penny saved is a penny earned," "Idle hands are the devil's workshop," and "Work before play," we *emphasize* hard work and material gain while *minimizing* the loss of our humanity in the process. When our bodily instincts and souls cry out in pain, we are called "crybabies" and "sissies." Through role modeling and this simple system of reward and punishment, we learn and teach how to desensitize ourselves to our humanity in order to grab the brass ring of societal approval. Under this complex system of societal gardening, our most beautiful flowers and nutritious vegetables are stamped out, while our weeds are cultivated and fertilized.

As an Ohio farm boy, for example, I showed an early aptitude for spirituality, psychology, music, and literature, but very little for farmwork and mechanics. I was extremely emotional and affectionate, liking nothing better than reading a good book or singing to myself or to whomever would listen. I also, however, craved love and approval. And in my culture, boys were praised and admired for their size, strength, athletic ability, and hard work. Sing for the cows if you want, but be out in the barn at sunup if you want approval. If you're good at reading, read this tractor manual and get the darned thing running. And if you like praying so much, ask God to bring us some rain before the crops fail. Now quit whining and get to work.

I learned well how to deaden the troublesome sensitivities that brought me punishment. When I asked to learn a musical instrument, my mother said it was "either music or basketball," and I chose basketball, a sport that was honored right up there with hard work in my family. When I began to work in the hayfields, I won high praise for saving money by letting my hands bleed and callous into unfeeling blobs during the first weeks of the season so that I would not need expensive gloves. I learned even at twelve years of age to work harder and longer than any "hired city boy," even if he were five years my senior. And like most boys, I learned to ignore my emotions and to sacrifice my body and soul as an unspoken rite of passage to my culture's version of manhood. Born during World War II, I was reared to believe in the glory of dying for my country. By the time I graduated from high school during the Vietnam era, I couldn't wait to join the army with my friends to sacrifice my life for my country. I was raised for sacrifice. It was the American way.

Having learned well how to ignore my mind/body's signals, I went on to test its endurance even more as an adult. I became a heavy drinker, and after nightly bouts of alcohol and too little sleep, I would have several cups of black coffee, smoke cigarettes, and eat sugar-laden donuts the next morning to overcome sleep deprivation and exhaustion. This cycle of abuse continued for years. Like Lynne, above, I hated my job and felt powerless to find more fulfilling work. Filled with drugs—alcohol, nicotine, caffeine, and sugar—all of my waking hours, I managed to repress the pain of body, emotions, and soul for years.

Farmers are a vanishing breed. I have none today as students or clients. But the traits I learned on the farm I see in people everywhere. Most of the people who come to me are from backgrounds very different from my own; many of them are from wealthy and sophisticated families and have been educated at prestigious universities.

Surely, I once thought, these educated and wealthy people would be spared the soul loss I suffered on the farm. Unfortunately, I found that they often have it much worse. While I was not expected to do well in school—education being a luxury in my family—these people were expected to excel. *Their* "hard work" was education and material success, and it began at birth. While I had some freedom of choice about what to do with my life, they had none. It was succeed professionally or be shamed and humiliated. Many of my less-advantaged friends and I were rebellious in school and avoided studying. Although we received our own kind of imbalance, we thank our lucky stars that we thus avoided the unhealthy one-sidedness we see in our clients and patients who spent their childhoods absorbed in studying and little else. Having succeeded in school and career, they are failing to have a full life.

Parents of these "privileged" people began researching prestigious preschools while Junior was still in the womb, which is today no refuge from language and music tapes played by parents anxious to give their children a "head start on the competition." I encounter many people like Clyde who are so inured to pressures of striving and competing that stopping to learn about themselves is absolutely terrifying, as if such oddities as body and spirit were taboo in their religion of material success. Consequently, their bodies are often twisted and dis-eased by the lifelong practice of tension and repression. With a lot of encouragement, Clyde has learned to heal his rift with Self by listening to his body and finding his own path. It is toward this path of Self-healing that I direct all people who seek me out.

Healing versus Fixing: The Ramifications of Imbalance

The greatest price we pay for the rift with Self described above is living with it. Like roses that never fully bloom, we are incomplete beings, still in the stem, proudly waving our unblossomed selves on the breeze without even the awareness of our incompleteness. Yet in my experience, most people are not aware of the great soul pain this condition exacts because we are completely unacquainted with our souls. Instead, we experience this pain as symptoms in our bodies or our emotions, and then only because the condition becomes so exacerbated that we cannot ignore it. Then we want to "fix it" as soon as possible, to cut it out like a bad weed with nary a thought for the imbalanced field in which it grew.

We seldom see our dis-ease as having anything to do with us or the way we live our lives, let alone as a symptom of our imbalance. Society—itself imbalanced—presents us with few lenses through which to observe its effects on us, and the people assigned to help us often see worse than we. It is a case of the blind leading the blind. When we become ill, we go to a modern doctor to get "fixed." We don't expect to hear a whole-person analysis, an assessment of our relationship with our soul, which could lead to our actually healing the rift with Self that may have spawned our illness. And we don't get it. With a few—but a rapidly growing number of—exceptions, modern medicine remains essentially soulless, a ramification of societal imbalance that leaves most ill people in the hands of clinicians who seldom see beyond symptoms.

Traditional healers, on the other hand, have known for thousands of years that the rift with Self and God are the same, and they seldom consider any aspect of our humanness as separate from any other part. A broken arm is not *just* a broken arm. If we look closely at how it happened and at the context of our lives at the time, we might discover the area where we were in disharmony with the Self and with God. Yes, the arm needs to be set and will gradually heal, but if we have the courage to ask, "Why did this happen?" we can perhaps strip away the veils of our everyday, business-as-usual perceptions and rediscover what our lives are really about. Then, and only then, can real healing— the return to harmony—take place.

The often told story of "The Sage and the Professor" exemplifies this approach: The sage and the professor were walking across a university campus when two bricks fell from a building top, brushing each person's right arm. The professor, who was overcome first with fear and then with rage, picked up the brick and began waving it angrily in the air. Then began a long pilgrimage, first to the provost office to complain about the incident, then to maintenance to rage and demand repairs, then to the dispensary to see if the brush had caused any damage he had not felt, and then to his attorney's office to see if he could gain any advantage in a lawsuit. He was bent on *fixing* the problem of falling bricks and could be heard for days afterward around campus ranting about the incident.

The sage? She simply picked up the brick and took it home to her meditation chamber. There she spent hours contemplating her relationship to herself and the universe, asking what if anything in her life was so out of balance as to require such a drastic incident to get her attention. And she gave sincere thanks for the fact that the brick had not killed her. She was bent not on *fixing* the falling-brick problem but on learning about herself.

Fixing is a mechanical concept based on a materialistic and mechanistic view of the world: Something breaks, fix it as you would a car, and forget it. The professor was definitely a fixer. The primary modern methodology, *fixing* deals with discrete parts of the human machine, often without considering the other parts or the whole. *Healing*, on the other hand, is a holistic proposition: Everything is part of the whole. Everything has meaning. Disharmony breeds harm. The sage was, of course, a natural healer.

Wellness in mind and body is the natural state of being, and so when illness of any kind strikes, it may be an indication that something is out of balance within the Self. Acknowledging that the battle for the Self must be won through integration, the sage might say that the arm will be fixed, but healing will happen only when the message of the Self is heard and acknowledged.

During my seven-year stint as a factory worker in Dayton, Ohio, I developed a debilitating back problem, which left me constantly bent like a pretzel. My medical doctor pronounced it a muscle strain and put me in a brace for six weeks, to no avail. Finally, against dire warnings from my physician, I decided to "jump paradigms" into the holistic world and visited a chiropractor, who had me vertical in one visit.

But this chiropractor did far more than fix my back. He began the process of healing my rift with God. He recognized something in me that was not compatible with factory work and convinced me to go to college, which I did the following year at the age of twenty-five. I have learned over the years since that incident to consider my back a good and trusted friend that will tell me, sometimes painfully, when I am out of sorts with my soul. My first chiropractor initiated that relationship by looking beyond mere symptoms and encouraging me to heal my life as well as my aching back. I count both my back problem and Dr. Lloyd as healing gifts from the universe, gifts from the soul. Together they literally changed the course of my life.

It is the very nature of our being to heal its rifts and become whole. All of being is involved in that process. Healing is therefore essential to all being; it is the very process of becoming whole. Natural healers know this basic truth and never try to *make* something happen. They simply look for and sense what is already in the process of happening and help it along. Doctor Lloyd sensed that my back problem was part of something which was "already happening" in my being and guided me to college, an environment he hoped would nurture its unfoldment in my life.

Many people blame our modern medical establishment for its frag-
mented approach to health. Being but a part of the societal mosaic,
however, it is not to blame. Medical people simply do what they are
trained to do and do it very well—*fix* people rather than *heal* them.
What they accomplish is absolutely miraculous. I would see them
immediately for a burst appendix or heart attack. But modern medical
people are not trained to see humans as complex, integrated systems
of wholeness, bound together and directed by an integrating intelligence. They are trained to be specialists, to see a biomechanical system
of parts, and to fix those parts when they demonstrate recognizable
symptoms. Practitioners trained in the modern medical tradition are
part of a scientific material society that sees only the obvious, the
material facade of things. They do what they are trained to do and
cannot be expected to do what they do not know.

Alternative and holistic heathcare practitioners are much more
likely to consider whole-person factors such as the soul and to
attempt healing rather than merely fixing. As a founding member of a
holistic health clinic that freely integrates the best of what works in
Eastern, Western, and alternative healthcare, I am often asked why
modern medical practitioners don't embrace the same perspective—
whatever works to help people heal. I tell them that it is a work in
progress. Deep change is slow, but it is happening. All of the practitioners at our clinic, Integrated Healing Arts, are active spiritual seekers. Several of them participate in our meditation classes, where we
are joined by physicians, nurses, teachers, and other professionals.
This is a society that is turning to wholeness, and professionals like
these will be teaching the next generation of physicians and teachers
about wholeness and healing.

Even as I write these words, I am on an airplane, returning from
teaching Process Acupressure, a mind/body/spirit discipline, to
licensed helpers educated in the modern healthcare model. My heart
has been touched by my students, many of whom made life-changing
breakthroughs in their personal and professional lives during the
course of the class. I remember faces, shining spirits, and bright eyes.
I recall one talented physical therapist in her early thirties whose self-

diagnosis of a severe rash was that she was "unable to express any negative feelings. I have smiled and taken it so long, I no longer know how
to have fun." After a weekend of acupressure, emotional release, love,
and meditating with her soul, her rash was gone, and she didn't expect
it to return. And after a weekend of listening to the deep whispering
of her Self, she felt healed enough to keep on listening. That's the
key—to keep on listening.

"I am so happy to hear you confirm what I've always known," she
said. "They told me in school I was too emotional and should keep my
objectivity, not care so much for my patients, just do my work and go
home. I began to feel that compassion was a handicap and that spirituality has no place in healing. I now feel like someone has taken the
chains off me. Now I can do my real work."

My niece, who lives in the region and is considering a career in
healthcare, asked what I was teaching and to whom. When I told her I
was teaching these holistic skills to health professionals, she said, "You
mean they don't know that? You mean they aren't taught that in training?" She was shocked. To her it was absurd that practitioners would be
trained to avoid emotions should they arise, to ignore a patient's
mental state, to ignore family and social influences, and to ignore the
yearnings of the soul. The professionals who come to my classes, and
others like them, are of the same opinion and are dedicated to learning
how to heal their own rifts with Self so that they can help heal their
clients and patients. A dream, years ago, told me that the most effective
way to help was to "teach the teachers," who will eventually heal the
imbalance in society. Today, that dream has become a reality for me.

Almost every one of my students after this recent class stopped to
tell me of a profound shift in perspective. A psychologist who had
been "locked up with a mean and punishing God for the past fifty
years" said, "I got so mad every time the nuns in the convent where I
was raised said Christ loved me, right after they told me what a
sinner I was. They convinced me I had betrayed him, little as I was.
I turned away from all of it. I think I've broken through this time,
though. I think I've got a feeling for my own inner God, and I don't
need theirs anymore.

"I woke up this morning with this clear thought, this clear under-standing that I've never had in all these years: 'If He died for my sins, that was his decision, not mine. No one asked me about it, and I'm not feeling guilty about it anymore.' That was it. My soul is free and I don't have to carry that cross around on these twisted old shoulders any-more. I'm free."

The ramifications of being raised in a society innately wounding to the Self are very great—especially when its anointed helpers are symptom fixers rather than whole-person healers. But the times they are a-changin'. I, too, was "locked in my head" when I began my work, and it was years before I learned that to truly heal, one must somehow navigate beneath the layers upon layers of metaphoric symptoms to hear the soul's urgent cry: "I am in pain. I am lonely. I am loveless, empty, and unfulfilled. Hear me and release me from these bonds. And in the process you will find that you and I are one."

LEARNING TO "READ GOD'S LIPS"

Many of us, reared with the fixer's mind-set, find it hard to compre-hend that healing the rift with Self is often synonymous with healing that greater rift. To us, an ulcer is only an ulcer, and will you please just fix the darned thing! But we're willing to learn how to heal our rifts, if someone will teach us to think in metaphoric rather than literal terms—a necessary skill if we are to understand the soul, which seldom speaks in discursive, "this is the way it is" language.

Ronald was just such a literal but willing-to-learn man. Even when his holistic doctor referred him to me "to see what you're doing to irri-tate that ulcer," he couldn't believe he had anything to do with his body's symptoms. It was while helping him that the term *reading God's lips* came to mind as a way to interpret what's happening in life from a healing perspective.

Ronald was a true literalist. If I told him that childhood wounds were like toxic dumpsites in our psyches, he would give me a blank stare. "What do you mean by that?" he'd ask, picturing little pockets and holes in his brain with oil and muck in them. And needless to say, his concept of the Divine was the paternalistic God in the sky, vehemently denouncing "bad" and rewarding "good" in his "children." Ronald was very devout, but he expected to find his answers "written in the holy book," not inscribed on the substance of everyday life. Helping him to understand that listening to his body and emotions might assist him in healing his ulcer and living more fully—let alone being closer to God—seemed almost impossible.

Finally, when I said to him in exasperation, "Ronald, you've got to learn how to read God's lips," he sat up and took notice.

"What do you mean by that?" he asked, this time alert and present.

"Your view of God is that he's present all the time, that not a leaf falls without his knowledge, right?" He agreed. "Then I would like you to consider that every sensation in your body, every emotion, every movement, every dream, every person you meet, and everything else that happens in your world *might* be nonverbal guidance from God, and when you *notice* them, you are reading God's lips."

Ronald understood that metaphor completely and very soon began "reading God's lips" as a means for healing his rift with Self and God. It is a simple task, requiring only attention and a willingness to trust in the subjective experience of inner guidance. As advanced as modern science has become, it cannot tell us how to live our lives in harmony with our total being. Only we can do that—by becoming aware of the signals that are always present in our feelings, our symptoms, and our dreams. When we learn to listen, we will find an amazingly accurate and profound guidance system.

Many holistic teachers and practitioners teach empowerment as a key to health, emphasizing that awareness of one's bodily sensations—heartbeat, breathing, emotions in the body, dreams, instinctual reactions, intuitions, and body image—is vital to good health and personal empowerment. These healers obviously know how to read God's lips and are dedicated to teaching this skill to others. Perhaps one day all modern healthcare will be based on the motto "All healing is self-healing," as it is at our center in Palo Alto, and everyone will know how to read God's lips.

When we read God's lips, we consider everything in our lives as part of our movement to wholeness, including conflicts with others, accidents of any sort, and certainly something so intimate as an illness or body symptom. Much of this work is like exploring the gigantic core of an iceberg after we have become conscious of its tip—as Lynne knew that her knee hurt but had to explore to find the huge iceberg beneath it that was sabotaging her growth. In Arnold Mindell's *Process Oriented Psychology*, for example, an illness is considered a signal that an unconscious aspect of oneself is knocking on the door to conscious expression. It is a signal of growth trying to happen in any way it can.

The key to all of this is *awareness*, an important component of spiritual growth as well as total well-being. As it turns out, most of us are aware of very little within or about ourselves, and it is this lack of awareness and the caring that this awareness can bring which creates our rifts. When the sages of the East tell us to eat when we are hungry and drink when we are thirsty, they mean just what Western sages do when they say "Know thyself." Learn about your body and its needs. When I clench my teeth and form a fist while smiling at someone and denying that I am angry or upset, I am demonstrating a significant lack of awareness of my own inner process. I am apt to stuff my anger and continue to endure whatever situation is contributing to it because I am not fully aware of what is happening within and around me. Somehow in my life experience, I have learned to protect myself by shutting down my awareness. But when I learn to notice my anger and be truthful about it, I choose to become aware. I now must accept that something about myself, this person, or the situation is causing me distress and do something to relieve it. As I take action to care for my emotions and my body, I am in the active process of healing my rift with Self.

When the wounded person no longer seeks only to have someone "fix" his symptoms after they have manifested but is actively engaged in learning about himself and his relationship to his body and his life, he is as good as healed; the journey to Self and ultimately to God has begun. At Integrated Healing Arts, for example, we consider healing to be the point at which this process of self-healing begins. We have looked too long outside ourselves to authorities and material success for our answers. The Truth, as the mystics of the ages have told us, lies in our reclaiming our lost Selves.

A SUMMARY DREAM

A dream I had several years ago summarizes our collective dilemma very nicely. In the dream, I had been living in the hollow interior of a huge rock that rested at the edge of the ocean, when one day a new, younger man arrived to take over management of the rock, which seemed to be a place of study and learning. One of his first tasks was to tour the whole facility, and in the process of the tour, we walked down a sort of ramp to a huge chamber under my domain where the *skeleton people* lived. Although I knew they lived there, I had not thought much about it, as one doesn't in dreams, but this new younger man wanted to know all about them and tried to communicate with them. They just stared at him blankly as he talked, and he finally gave up and walked back toward the upper world, perhaps as others had before him.

As we walked away, I was suddenly struck with an inner urgency and a great idea. I walked back to the lower chamber, took a book from a large library there, and ran back to my new boss. I opened the book to show him pages of picture stories and symbols, which neither of us understood. But as we read, we looked up to see that the leader of the skeleton people was very interested in what we were now doing—he had ignored us before—and had followed to tell us something. Although we could not make out any words, we understood his message: "We want to communicate with you, but *your* language is far too limited for our use. You must learn our language of symbols. Then you will understand."

From the point of that dream, I knew that my life's purpose required that I learn this basic language of the body—and soul. As Dr. Fritz Smith, author of *Inner Bridges* and founder of the soul bodywork Zero Balancing, told me, "This dream gave you a mission." The soul, as we have seen, speaks through the body and emotions as well as through the language of dreams and myth. Experiences with myself and hundreds of others teach me that our souls speak to us through those media all the time, calling us back to our true nature. As my dream put it, we "must learn our language of symbols," including body/mind symptoms and events in our lives, to understand what our souls have to tell us about our real Self and how to heal our rift with it. To do so is requisite to healing our rifts with God.

~ 3 ~

THE FIVE WOUNDS YOUR
DOCTOR WILL NEVER FIND

MOST OF US HAVE HAD THE EXPERIENCE of buying a car we had not previously noticed on the road, only to see that model everywhere we went from the moment we started driving it. This happens not only with cars, of course. It can happen in any area of life. We have an experience that opens our eyes to something we'd not previously noticed. Then suddenly we're seeing it everywhere. It is almost as if the invisible were made visible through some magic process.

That's the way it was for me when I began working with people after the soul-awakening experience in Utah. Everywhere I looked after that, I found people with the same soul sickness I had before my own breakthrough. I would bang my head with my hands in disbelief: Is this real or am I only projecting onto the world like any new convert? Both cases were true, of course. What I was suddenly seeing for the first time had been there all along, but I could see it only after I had been through the fire of spiritual recovery—and only then with the help of the clients and students whose recovery depended upon being seen and understood.

The people most helpful in the early stages of this process were participants in a weight-reduction clinic I directed about fifteen years ago in Los Altos, California. A holistic program, my clinic helped clients and students study their whole lives in order to understand their eating compulsions. Compulsive eating—like everything else—does not happen in a vacuum but is intimately interwoven with the rest of our lives, including our childhood issues, our relationships, our attitudes, and our soul wounds.

One evening during group discussion, the subject of God came up. Greta, a large, quiet soul who seldom spoke, took a deep breath and blew our group into uncharted waters. Greta said that she believed her real hunger was for God, that food was only a poor substitute, and that she had no idea how to satisfy her real hunger because she would never go back to the church in which she was raised. That single comment launched a lively discussion that would last for weeks and change our group forever.

"I don't want to bring God into this," asserted Ethel, a normally quiet and noncommittal woman who always sat by the door, looking as though she might bolt at any moment. "I've had enough of God to last a lifetime."

"Yeah, me too," said Fred, a man in his forties who so adamantly insisted on his atheism that we all wondered what lay behind it. "I don't want this to turn into another Alcoholics Anonymous meeting where we all have to surrender to this *God thing*. I wouldn't do it for them, and I won't do it for you."

Everyone quickly agreed that we would leave God out of our discussions, since the subject made everyone so uncomfortable, but then we proceeded to discuss how much this *God thing* had created pain and unbalance in our lives. It seemed perfectly OK to discuss God, as long as we agreed that it wasn't a part of the official program and that no one would try to convert anyone else to his or her beliefs. In fact, we had nothing to worry about in this regard; it was several weeks before anything positive was said about past religious experiences.

The depth and power of the discussions that followed astonished me. Here was a group of people, gathered to heal weight problems, who found in the process that the wounds causing them to overeat against their will were rooted in painful rifts with a God that many of them had long ago banished from their lives. One by one, in this loving setting where they did not *have* to discuss God, these people talked about him to exhaustion. They disclosed to themselves and others the great emptiness inside that could not be filled with food. They talked about yearning to belong, to feel a part of something greater than themselves, but being blocked by their past experiences with religion. They talked about vicious nuns, fanatical parents, sexual abuse by priests; they discussed stifling dogma, damaging guilt and shame, and rigid structures that threatened their individuality and creativity; they complained of hypocritical parishioners, seductive rabbis, sadistic teachers, atheistic parents, the narrowing nature of science, and obsessive materialism. They talked and listened and then talked some more until they could find nothing more to say.

By the time we were finished, I understood why it was necessary that we talk: we were all wounded. We all had rifts with God, which had never been addressed in our religious or therapeutic communities. Our religions, those institutions designated to help us relate to God, tended to act like co-abusers instead of our protectors, defending the system that perpetrated our wounding. And the physicians and therapists we often turned to for help with our spiritual wounds were trained in a scientific materialism that refused to recognize the soul. We, in that little group, listened to each other and helped each other heal. Surprisingly, we all lost weight in the process! But more important was what we *gained*—a clear picture of our deepest wound, our rift with God, and a supportive system to help us heal it.

THE FIVE TYPES OF WOUNDS

The weight-control group was but one source of the five types of wounds I found. My clients and other students over the years helped me refine and clarify these types. In the early years of my career I taught many classes on habit control and helped people deal with addictions of various sorts. I heard these people echo over and over the addictive statement of Saint Paul: "That which I would do I do not do; and that which I would not do, I do." I kept asking them and myself, "What is this great thirst or hunger we've all described within us that is never satisfied? What do we want?" Or in the words of Ochwiay Biano, "What are they seeking?" As I kept searching for the answer, I gradually identified the five key types of wounds involved.

The five types are *recovering from religion*, *recovering from rebellion against religion*, *recovering from God-betrayal*, *recovering from scientific materialism*, and *recovering from nothingness*. The first three types describe people who have been directly injured by affiliations with institutional religion and its representatives or by a violation of their faith that they blamed on God. Members of the last two types—*recovering from scientific materialism* and *recovering from nothingness*—were robbed of their souls through other social forces.

RECOVERING FROM RELIGION

The weight group, as it turned out, was full of people who were recovering from religion. I found that out when we were discussing the kinds of hunger we try to satisfy with food, such as hunger for love, affection, mental stimulation, sensuality, or sex. Everyone could relate to these problems except Helen, a meek, recently divorced woman in her late forties who kept shaking her head that none of these applied to her. I finally stopped the class to ask about her own particular issue.

"I do well with weight until Sunday," she said, ducking her head into her hands briefly, as if trying to hide from our inquiries.

"Why Sunday?" I asked.

"I don't know. I guess I have more time on my hands."

"But wait a moment," I prompted. "You work at home. Why Sunday instead of Saturday, or Tuesday, for that matter?"

Again, the hiding gesture. "I guess it's church," she said, reluctantly. "Right after mass I start eating and eat all day. I don't know why."

I poked and prodded for a while longer, feeling rather inadequate for not understanding what Helen was trying to say, when Margaret interjected a thought that abruptly cleared up the issue for us all: "It's communion, isn't it?"

I had no clue about communion, but Margaret, an assertive, dark-haired woman who was always certain she knew what she was talking about, certainly did. I knew that both of them were Catholic, and I saw that Helen dropped her eyes to the floor when Margaret spoke. She seemed close to tears.

"Is Margaret right about communion, Helen?" I asked, touching her shoulder. "I don't know much about Catholics and communion. I was raised a Methodist."

Helen wouldn't talk. She slowly placed her arms under her breasts and almost imperceptibly began to rock her body, like a child in pain comforting herself. A big wave of emotion was gathering just beneath her surface, ready to burst, but as yet Helen was holding it back, realizing perhaps that once the dike broke, the waters they held would wash away untold inner structures. She was afraid to see what she had sought so hard to find. I had no idea what the issue was, but Margaret knew very well and was more than happy to share it.

"It's communion. I know it," she said firmly, her large head nodding affirmatively. "It almost killed me when I first got divorced, too. I'd eat all day."

"But why? What's divorce got to do with communion?" I asked. "Does the church bar you from communion just because you're divorced? And why do you care?"

At this point both women looked at me reproachfully, and I shrank back. We had joked many times that I must have been a priest in a past life, because most of the group members were Catholic and I filled that role for them, but I now felt my lack of instruction for the job. I had studied the Catholic ritual of the Eucharist in graduate school to understand Irish literature, and I knew the importance placed on confession and communion. But something was missing in the puzzle. Why was Helen so distraught? Margaret, of course, soon enlightened me.

"There's no rule that you can't take communion if you're divorced," she said. "But they ruin it for you. The church tells you that marriage is for life, and all the priests and nuns let you know there's no excuse for divorce. If the spouse has affairs or is an alcoholic or beats you, you're supposed to talk it over with a priest and live with it. Even if they leave you, you're at fault because you failed in some way. You've sinned somehow, and there's nothing you can do about it. People pull away from you a little bit. Even old friends and family don't know what to do with you, because the reality of your experience doesn't match the fantasy even you believed before it happened to you. Unless it has happened to them, they don't understand because they believe what they've been taught—that *good* Catholics don't get divorced. You feel like an outsider. Like a pariah. And you don't just take the sacrament like nothing has changed. Even I didn't, and I'm stubborn as hell. You just don't!"

"That's right. You don't," Helen echoed, sobbing openly now that her shame was known. "Divorce just isn't supposed to happen in the Catholic Church. They think if they start accepting it as something that happens, the gates of hell will open and everybody will start doing it. So they just pretend it doesn't happen and on we go. All I know is I can't walk up there and take communion like a good Catholic when I'm treated like I don't deserve it. I'm thinking of quitting the church, but what would I do with myself after all these years?"

Helen cried until she was dry, and many of us cried with her. It is a sacred moment when our wounds are revealed to others who understand and hold our pain with us. Helen was what I call a "true believer," a characteristic of wounded religionists. She and others like her are the innocent sheep who trust the shepherd all the way to the slaughterhouse. They believe in the dogma of their religions; they obey all the rules and do everything they are told; they believe that the road to heaven and peace on earth is paved by following all the rules laid down by the saintly institutions and their infallible representatives. While other members of their parishes take it all with a cynical eye, winking smugly as they break all the rules, these innocents believe and obey. They believe with their ministers that bad things don't happen to good people, even when a bad thing happens to them. And when they get bitten by the very dog they trusted to protect them, they are injured to the quick.

Yet, wounded as they are, they remain true to the faith. Many continue to attend church or temple. Others stop attending but remain true believers in their hearts. But like the faithful child who remains loyal to an abusive parent, they do so at their souls' expense. The bandage needs to be torn from the infected wound and the scab removed so it can heal from the inside.

As is happening everywhere with sexual abuse, the spiritually abused must confront their abusers and make a new covenant between them if they are to have a healthy relationship, or else these wounded souls must find some other way to heal and relate to their divinity. If the wound remains unrecognized and untended, these true believers will remain in the painful limbo of the rift—and continue to labor under the cruel master of separation from God.

Recovering religionists come in assorted packages: Fundamentalist Christians who feel like sinners because they like to dance or have sex; Jews who have married out of their religion; Catholics who defy the pope's stand on birth control. Their connecting link is an unshakable belief that the rules and ministers are right and they are wrong—that they are not *good* Christians, Catholics, Jews, Muslims, or whatever. Therefore, they feel unworthy, and they turn their faces away from God.

These people may be no more conscious of what happened to them than was Helen, but they are wounded all the same. The most innocent and faithful among us, they are lost to themselves—and God. And the only way back from that purgatory of the soul is to recognize and heal the rift with God, whether it takes them back to confront and engage their own religions or to string their own deal with the Almighty by finding God on their own, beyond the walls of the institutions.

This last alternative—to find God through personal experience—is the ultimate healing for all spiritual wounds. Everybody has to do it sooner or later, because belief in a dogma or an institution is not necessarily a belief in God. This is the blessing of spiritual woundedness: it forces us to step away for a while from the comfort of our religious habit of simple faith in the institution, to find God in the mystery of our own hearts. We get the opportunity to grow up, to mature spiritually.

RECOVERING FROM REBELLION AGAINST RELIGION

Rebels against religion are as much true believers as religionists. But they don't take their wounds lying down. They're fighting mad about it.

Take Dan, for example. When he first visited me for a relationship issue, he was furious with God, who by the way didn't exist as far as he was concerned. A small man with a power about him that filled the room, Dan hated God for "giving me a religion that screwed me up with women."

"Here I am in love with another unavailable woman," he ranted. "Hell, I know what that's about. They raised me as an altar boy, groomed me for the priesthood. But I like women and sex too much for that. I'm not gonna do it! But every woman I fall in love with is unavailable to me. It's like they're gonna make me live like a priest whether I like it or not. Well, to hell with them! I'm not going to do it."

Dan had an incongruence in his presentation that I had grown accustomed to in religious rebels. He had intellectually decided he was an atheist but was still "mad as hell at Him." He couldn't see that to be mad at God is to believe there is a God. Dan *believed*, obviously, but he rebelled against believing because his belief caused him the intolerable pain of being alone, without the soul mate he so desired. He had read all the relationship-addiction books, had been through a program or two, and had pursued counseling. But it all had served only to convince him that it was the nonexistent God's fault for declaring him a priest.

Dan was a true believer, and it drove him crazy because he didn't want to be one. Strong-willed and stubborn, he turned his back on the devotional part of himself and decided it didn't exist. That, as any counselor can tell you, is a blueprint for big problems.

I identified with Dan from the moment we met. I, too, had for years entertained an intellectual arrogance that I could decide whether or not God exists. Like a flea on the dog that decided there was no dog, I decided in the middle of my junior year at college that God was no more than a figment of ignorant people's imaginations, and I flicked him out of existence. Like Dan, I had always been an innocent, a true believer. For me, as for him, it was spiritual suicide to eliminate my connection to divinity. Therefore, helping Dan had that extra edge which made his recovery especially important to me.

As it turned out, Dan's self-assessment was well off the mark. In fact, the unavailable women to whom he was attracted were not God's revenge for his not becoming a priest. Instead, he gradually discovered that they were renditions of his own rejecting and vicious mother, who constantly used withholding of love as a weapon to make him excel as a student and future priest. As we explored his anger at his mother for her malicious manipulation, Dan discovered a long-locked-up secret that he did not want to see: as an altar boy, Dan had been molested by the church's most holy priest, Dan's idol. He never reported it to anyone, and the event had remained like a charred stake in his devotional heart all these years, forbidding any light or love to enter its shamed chambers. In that child's heart he had always believed himself unholy and unworthy, somehow to blame for the priest's evil, and doomed by his sexual urges to follow in his perpetrator's footsteps if he were to become a priest. He felt trapped for God's unholy pleasure, like an animal in a cage, until he finally did what he had to for survival: he declared God dead.

As he unraveled the tangled web of his rift with God, Dan began to redirect his anger toward the real villain—his mother and the priest—and it then gradually dissolved. Over time he realized that the priesthood had been his true calling all along. But he now realized it in its larger sense—as a call to God. So long a rebel, he made peace with the Catholic Church and then set out on his own personal spiritual quest to heal his rift with God.

I have known hundreds of men and women like Dan over the years, people who rebel with anger against religion of all types and simultaneously rebel against God. It shows in their faces when anyone mentions God, religion, or faith. It's not simply a look of disinterest but a deep anger, a rage: "How dare you express that crap in front of me?" they seem to think. "I was injured by it. I was hurt. And I don't want to hear about it in any form."

Among these rebels you will find people of all religions and traditions: Jews taught Hebrew as children who won't allow a rabbi within a yard of them, angry that they were submitted to rigorous training in a faith their parents no longer followed; Christians who glare angrily at the wall when the family says grace at meals. Some of them still feel the rage from forced religious schooling and indoctrination, from being beaten by nuns or abused by ministers. Most are true believers who completely accepted what they were taught only to feel betrayed by God when the dogma proved untrue and their teachers proved hypocrites.

Yet as true believers, they have no choice but to look beyond their anger and engage the process of healing. They must learn as Dan and I did, each in their own way and time, that God is there forever, beyond form and structure, beyond dogma, ministers, rabbis, or gurus. It is the God within our own hearts that we must find and make peace with, for it was not God who inflicted our wounds but misguided human beings and our own inaccurate concepts about what God is and does.

RECOVERING FROM GOD-BETRAYAL

"Don't talk to me about God. God's given me nothing but grief, and I want nothing to do with him." Martin bounced up from his chair and strode toward the door. I thought for a moment he might walk out on me, but he only paced around for a moment and sat back down. I was both shocked and pleased by his outburst. He had come to me some weeks before to deal with a deep despair that several psychologists had not seemed to touch. Until that moment, he had answered all my questions in the same tired monotone, showing scant signs of the vibrant businessman he had been before the death of his son some five years before. For the first time he was showing signs of life. And all I had asked was, "Has your religion been any comfort to you with your son's death, Martin?"

Martin was Jewish, and although he had never been one to "run to the rabbi with every problem," he was a true believer. He came from a good family, was brought up in a good neighborhood in New York City, was given an excellent education, and took over a flourishing family business that he expanded beyond anyone's expectations. He had married a beautiful and successful woman he loved deeply and had two sons and a daughter he adored. Until his younger son's death, he had been very active in charity and community work, giving "back to God for his blessings to me."

Martin had felt a powerful bond with God, a strong covenant. Everything good in his life he believed came from God. And when his youngest son died, he believed that also came from God. And it was too much for him to bear. As far as Martin was concerned, his covenant with God was broken by that death. He felt betrayed by God.

How strange, I thought, as he stormed to me about his anger with God, that no one had asked him this simple question about his covenant. He wouldn't volunteer it, of course, to anyone who would not understand his "simple" faith. He had long been accustomed to hiding it from his cynical friends for whom such spiritual trust was outdated. Certainly he wouldn't share it when his anger and pain were too great to hide with a flippant comment such as "I believe in God just in case I'm wrong and there is someone there after all." I knew that on some level he was guided to me because I would hear him as he needed to be heard—because I, too, am a man of simple faith, a true believer.

Like Job of the Hebrew scriptures, Martin needed not to be lectured to by well-meaning believers but to fight it out with God. A rabbi friend of mine likes to say that one is never closer to God than when disputing angrily with Him. Martin had turned away from God in anger, like a hostile spouse choosing to punish with silent reproach. His outburst to me was Martin's first foray into a first-rate battle with God that ended, along with his grief, in full reconciliation. Today, Martin's relationship with God is stronger than ever because it is established on the bedrock of acceptance. Death, too, is a part of life. And just because we don't understand them doesn't mean we are betrayed when unpleasant things happen.

So it goes with recovering from God-betrayal. Many of the people I've met carried their sense of betrayal from childhood, when a parent or favorite pet was killed, when an uncle molested them, or when their fervent prayers weren't answered. Children aren't stupid. If you tell them that God is real and answers their prayers, but no matter how hard they pray, Mommy and Daddy never get back together, they eventually draw their own conclusions: God has betrayed them for some reason. It happens with grownups like Martin, too. When something hurtful enough happens that doesn't fit into their picture of the way God should treat them, they get mad. That's it! They throw God out of their lives like an unfaithful spouse.

Of course their view of divinity is very limited and simple. But it is also beautiful and sincere. No frail-hearted cynics, these God-betrayal folks. And after they get back in relationship with God, perhaps through the help of a good counselor, and express their feelings with God face-to-face, magical things happen for them. A relationship is often forged that can withstand the tempests of disappointment and pain. The rift with God becomes a bridge to deep spiritual love and transcendence. This is a pattern in healing rifts with God: *The wound becomes the main thoroughfare to a deeper, more mature relationship with the divine, one that can withstand the ebb and flow of material fortune.* Even pain and death are a part of God's benevolence for one whose rift with God is healed.

RECOVERING FROM SCIENTIFIC MATERIALISM

In a sense, all of us are in the process of recovering from scientific materialism, for it is the context, the milieu, in which we were reared. Almost all of us were raised by rational materialists, educated by them, married them, are employed by them, and have them as friends. We *are* them in a very real sense. Like fish in water, we cannot help but be influenced by the medium in which we live.

Scientific materialism is the religion of the twentieth century. We all know that any religion is but a point of view, a belief system, a way of looking at the universe and its workings, a way of explaining what is so. The *science* in the term refers to scientific methodology, which says in short that nothing exists unless it is *proven* to exist under controlled, repeatable laboratory conditions. *Materialism*, the second aspect of the dogma, refers to the value system our society embraces, which as Webster points out, insists that "everything in the world, including thought, will, and feeling, can be explained only in the terms of matter."

Scientific materialism is the most powerful tool known to humankind. Without it we could not have come close to making the atomic bomb, the television, or any of the wonders of our age. It is the child of our reason, one of our most marvelous human faculties. And used

as that—one of our faculties in service to the Self—it is to be cele-
brated as a true gift to human nature. Only when it becomes a religion
and is elevated as the *supreme universal truth*, the scale on which all existence must be tested for validity, does it overreach itself and become a
scourge on humanity and a means of its destruction.

When I first started college at the age of twenty-five, I was somehow naive enough to expect scientific materialism to prevail only in
subjects conducive to scientific methodology, such as chemistry, math,
and physics. I did not dream for a moment that it would also be used
to interpret and evaluate the arts, literature, psychology, religion, and
philosophy. I was a literature major and expected freedom to study and
enjoy poetry for its beauty of form and spiritual feeling. What I got was
scientific materialism—fruit of the spirit reduced to the petri dish of
scientific analysis. Literature, art, religion, and philosophy were not to
be enjoyed but to be analyzed and criticized, tested and reported on
like so many chemicals in a test tube. Today, learning has become synonymous with the rational-material approach to life. And like the fundamentalist believer of any faith who declares that no one can get to
God except through his faith, scientific materialists declare that one
has not learned literature, or any other subject, unless he has been
tempered in the fire of scientific-material philosophy.

In my experience, one who totally surrenders his life to the
scientific-material dogma has a severe rift with God. How can it be
otherwise when the highest aspects of human experience—love,
spirituality, creativity, compassion—transcend material life? A belief
system is a lens through which we gaze at our world, a lens which
automatically filters out phenomena that contradict our belief's basic
assumptions. I have personally witnessed miracles happen before the
eyes of scientific materialists only to have them rationalize the event
away in order to maintain their dogma.

George, a friend of mine, was a man with a rift with God so severe
that he could not contain a condescending sneer whenever one of his
friends mentioned experiences or opinions contrary to his beliefs.
To be sure, he held his tongue most of the time. He had to because we
were all outside his faith with our involvement in transpersonal

psychology, spirituality, and holistic health. He was outnumbered, so he would hold his tongue. But he let us know in various ways how disgusted he was with our shoddy, unscientific approach to life.

One day a severe heart attack changed all that. When I next saw him I was amazed at his transformation. Psychologists, ministers, and holistic-health folks are quite accustomed to this phenomenon. When faced with death or major illness, rigid scientific materialists—recognizing that their dogma offers no comfort—will often soften and open to alternative views. George had an added incentive: during his hospital stay, he had an out-of-body experience and several drug-induced visions of an afterworld, experiences that he eagerly shared with his "weird" friends who had been talking about such things for years. He even began seeing a psychologist, "to see if there's anything to this repressed-emotions-causing-physical-problems stuff."

For a while, George was a mystic. When we friends got together, he was in the middle of all our conversations, sharing his dreams, talking about his breakthroughs in therapy, and asking our opinions about his spiritual experiences. We were amazed at his apparent transformation.

But as he got physically healthier, George became more unhealthy spiritually. When some three months had passed, he came to a party at my house. After the usual inquiries about his health, I asked about his therapy and growing spirituality. "Oh, that," he said, with the familiar contemptuous curl to his lip. "I got into that because of my 'holy vision.' I've gotten over that now. My doctor assured me that a lot of people hallucinate under those medications."

What George's doctor failed to point out was that "hallucinations" often contain the seeds of truth and spiritual growth. But his doctor's comment was opening enough for George to escape. He was in fact worse than ever. Instead of silently sneering, he became openly angry and insulted us to the point that we stopped talking about such things in his presence and eventually stopped seeing him altogether. He had returned to his scientific-material belief system with a vengeance, and any talk that contradicted it was unbearable to hear.

The Chinese have a saying: "Where there is a front, there's a back: big front, big back." George's illness put him in touch with the huge "back" to his belief system, and rather than face it head-on he decided on some level to grow a huge "front" to counteract it. It cost him his friends, and he later died anyway, facing that huge "back" of the spirit world whether he liked it or not. We received a call from him on our phone machine some years ago, a week or so before his final heart attack. He wanted to see us, but we didn't respond immediately, wanting to avoid his acerbic wit as long as possible. The next we heard about George, he was dead.

Most of the people I know are recovering scientific materialists. I'm not sure anyone can get through our society and educational system without adopting the tenets of that "faith" to some degree. All of my students and clients are recovering, usually jolted into it by some event or illness.

Jim, a former engineer who has been teaching meditation with me for a decade, needed a triple-bypass to jolt him into recovery. Today, his fondest wish is to be able to take what he has learned back into the laboratories and corridors of Silicon Valley to save the suffering masses he has left behind. I'm afraid that his dream is in vain. Most of us require a major incident like Jim's or mine to shock us into recovery. And most engineers are dyed-in-the-wool scientific materialists, as are the doctors who fix them. Like George, they will in all likelihood remain so till the day they die. Let's pray that they transition a bit more gracefully than George.

RECOVERING FROM NOTHINGNESS

She was thirty-two years old when I first met her, a lovely blonde woman who seemed to have everything life could offer. She was married to a highly successful medical doctor from Stanford University, where she herself held an MBA. She seemed to be doing an excellent job of balancing marriage, the mothering of two healthy preschool-age children, and a dynamic career in computer sales. And she had recently been declared psychologically healthy by two psychologists and a Stanford psychiatrist. "So why, if I'm so damned healthy and successful," she asked me, "do I feel so empty and lost?"

Truthfully, Melanie threw me way off guard at first. I'm used to having materially successful people reveal a great emptiness in their hearts, but Melanie was such an extreme opposite from me that I could hardly believe her story.

People who were raised poor, like me, often have a blind spot. They tend to believe on some level that all "real" problems are money-related, as it had been for them, and that anyone born with that proverbial silver spoon has no "real" problems. Melanie looked that way to me. Reared by a pair of affluent Stanford scientists, she had the best life had to offer from the time she broke water, and she was still enjoying the milk and honey of life. The poor farm boy in my psyche whispered in my ear the same message the psychologists must have heard: "Who is this princess trying to kid? Snap out of it, lady. You've got it made."

My reaction lasted only a moment, until the genuine pain in Melanie's voice reminded me that the psychiatrist had sent her to me for the very purpose that there was no material or psychological reason for the painful heartache driving her to distraction. As I opened myself to that pain, feeling it in my own heart in order to understand, I almost wept with its immensity. I then knew her problem, more painful than any mere disorder: Melanie had no connection with her soul.

As she caught me up on her life to date, I slowly began to appreciate her predicament. She had been reared as a perfect child. Adjudged "mentally gifted" at an early age, she was given a tutor at three and placed in accelerated classes all through school. As Stanford scientists, her parents were so immersed in scientific materialism that they were not even dogmatic about it. "Why belabor the obvious?" they seemed to feel, and they had no need to be concerned, to be sure, since "all the best schools" in this region are appointed with devout scientific materialists as well.

The odd point is that Melanie, unlike most others in her situation, did not absorb that dogma as her own. Like many children who go to church schools without getting religious, she did not get the scientific-material message of her parents and affluent environment.

She had all the best that scientific materialism had to offer, but she was neither scientific nor material. Nothing she had meant anything to her—neither the money, the degrees, nor the status. She was the Princess of Nothingness. No one can understand emptiness more than a person who has everything but feels painfully empty inside. How horrible, after all, to have in other people's eyes no "reason" for being miserable.

Melanie was one of the most difficult people I have ever tried to help. She believed in nothing, and thus had nothing to hold on to. "Nothing comes from nothing," said Shakespeare's King Lear. According to her upbringing, even the concepts of soul and spirit were so outlandish as to be ridiculous. "Aren't these archaic and primitive beliefs, proven false long ago by the advent of science?" she asked, when I offered that her pain may have a spiritual origin.

"Educated people don't actually believe this rubbish, do they? I understand it to be a crutch grasped at by weak-minded people who want hope at any price. I'm certainly not that bad off."

What saved Melanie was beyond my talents. Frankly, I prayed for her. I simply asked that she find the truth that would set her free from her pain, whatever that may be and in whatever form she could accept. Prayers work. Even scientific materialists—ones in touch with their souls—have been proving this under laboratory conditions for a long time now. Melanie had a transformational dream about meeting her bright soul in the middle of a dark woods. She asked her soul why she was plagued with the awful pain in her heart, and her soul replied, "Because you won't believe in me."

Melanie changed virtually overnight. She asked me for spiritual guidance and for a way "to start believing in my soul." The door opened and she walked through. All she needed was willingness, and God did the rest. Melanie's advantage in all this was that once she broke through that initial barrier, she had none of the resistances and wounds of the other types mentioned above. As golf pros tell us, beginning players are much easier to teach and have infinite potential because they have "beginner's mind," free of the years of bad habits accumulated by more experienced players. Melanie's rift with God was actually healed with that dream. All that remained was filling in the blanks. She already had every material thing she could want; now she has the soul connection to enjoy it.

Melanie's recovery from nothingness is not an unusual phenomenon. I have encountered many people like her, rich and poor, successes and failures, churchgoers and atheists. The key characteristic of them all is that they function in the world but believe in nothing. "We are the straw men. We are the hollow men," wrote the poet T. S. Eliot. Peggy Lee's hauntingly empty rendition of "Is That All There Is?" also speaks to this prevalent issue in our culture. Perhaps we've all experienced it at one time or another, the empty sense of having no connection to the passion of our souls.

It was that same experience which drove me to college at twenty-five, to California at thirty, and to Utah at thirty-three. A person in pain keeps moving. I felt the same empty longing as Melanie, but unlike her I lacked things that kept me searching. When I became a scientific materialist in college, I got passionate, thinking I had found something to believe in. After that short-lived euphoria, California was liberating but not an answer to my emptiness. Utah and poetry were last-ditch efforts for me, but there I found what so many Melanies have found—not a destination but an inward journey that would heal my rift with God.

We may consider the category of recovering from nothingness to be interwoven into all the other types discussed above, because it speaks most directly to a dis-ease affecting our whole culture. Since our chief religion is scientific materialism—a philosophy that permeates our religions, educational systems, and economy—we can expect an epidemic of nothingness well into the twenty-first century. Scientific materialism has no soul, you see. It is beautiful and powerful as a tool of the total self. But when its proponents raise it up like a gold idol and declare that God is dead, they cast out all that's holy. When it usurps the throne of God, it no longer connects with our hearts, instincts, or intuition. It has no answer to the problem of death or the search for meaning and purpose in our lives. It fails even those who have made a religion of it and have succeeded in converting nearly every country on earth to its tenets. Since it has no soul, it can never help one heal the rift with God.

USING THE FIVE TYPES

We don't talk about spiritual wounds in our culture. You won't find discussions like this in psychology's diagnostic manual or in your physician's handbook. In all likelihood, even your spiritual advisor won't have a diagnostic tool for your spiritual dilemma. Yet any person who has struggled with chronic depression will tell you that it was helpful to know that he or she was depressed, not just lazy and stupid. Many recovering alcoholics will acknowledge that their recovery became possible only when they recognized their alcoholism and declared it before a company of others in the same stew. Telling others, as one of my students likes to say, dissolves the sense of separation between us and others and our God.

When we see that someone knows about our particular kind of pain and has established a way to describe it, we feel better about ourselves. It helps us recognize that we have reasons for being the way we are, that we are alright human beings. We have made the first step toward recovery, and perhaps the remainder of this book will widen that step into a path worth traveling.

In most cases I have encountered, awareness and acceptance have been major parts of the cure, especially when witnessed by one or more other people. Melanie, for example, in her recovery from nothingness, had no trouble with the job once she saw clearly in her dream that her loss of soul was at the root of her problem. By the same token, once rebel Dan saw that his anger toward God was deferred rage from his abusers within the church, he was halfway home.

The way to use these types, therefore, is to simply read their descriptions, recognize the truth about your own life and beliefs, and perhaps tell some people what you have learned. My experience with clients and students is that recognition comes quickly and easily. Most people, by the way, see themselves in more than one type. Each type in which they see themselves helps to flesh out and clarify the kind of wound they suffer. I, for example, see parts of myself in all five types of wounds.

So if you find yourself in more than one type, or even in all of them, what is your label? None. Typing is not about labeling. Rather, it's about learning who we are. It's merely a tool, a simplified step to help us understand where we are today and where we are headed. It's the map, not the journey, and not our ultimate destination. The path to healing begins with that first step of simply recognizing our hidden wounds. And that first step—like Dorothy's heel-clicking in *The Wizard of Oz*—magically transports us into another world where we are healing our rift with God.

— 4 —

THE FIVE STAGES TO
A HEALED LIFE

I MET WOLFGANG ON A TROOP SHIP headed for Germany. He was a
grown man in his thirties, while I was just eighteen years old. At
the time I thought we were equal friends. But as I look back on it now,
I see that he took me under his wing. I was an innocent farm boy away
from home for the first time on a U.S. Army mission to secure the
East-West German border, and he was a German national returning
to his home country as a U.S. soldier after many years abroad. This
journey across the North Atlantic was for me an initiation, for him
a completion.

The old World War II ship was slow, giving us many days and
nights to talk and share our excitement. We talked mostly about
Germany—how it differed from America and how one gets on there.
I asked questions and he talked. I was thrilled to have a native prepare me for the journey, while he seemed to know that our talks
helped him make sense of his long separation from his homeland and
his imminent return.

Wolfgang had left home at eighteen also, not long after the end of
World War II. West Germany was in the process of rebuilding, but he
had never felt a part of it. His father had died in the war, and he
adopted as his heroes the American soldiers who gave him candy and

played with him. His heart ached to leave home for glorious America, and as soon as he was old enough he did. He immigrated to Chicago, where he became a printer and later married an American woman named Patsy, whom he loved dearly. A few months after becoming an American citizen, he received his draft notice and volunteered to return to Germany.

"I tell you, Paul, there is God's hand in this," he told me as we sat on deck under the stars. "I have not been back home since I moved to America and would not be going now if not for the army. But it is right for me to be going home now. I can feel it. God has a reason for me to go back now. And I'm going home as an American soldier! Just like the men who were kind to me as a boy. What could be better!"

Wolfgang held a vision of those benevolent heroes of his youth, and this return as a U.S. soldier made him, in his mind, a returning hero, feared and respected by his countrymen. He pictured himself as a mediator between his two countries, telling his countrymen about America and his great adventures there and introducing American GIs to the German culture. His vision was clear. He knew who he was and what he was meant to do. I admired him greatly.

I like to remember Wolfgang from those shipboard days. Things got too confusing for us after we got ashore and to our unit. We drifted apart. I had all I could handle finding my place as a boy among men in a strange new outfit. And Wolfgang found himself far from being a returning hero and mediator. I watched him grow angry and bitter. He was treated with suspicion and scorn by both the villagers, who had grown tired of foreign soldiers on their soil, and by American soldiers, who made themselves comfortable seeing Germans as "Krauts"—unfriendly foreigners who overcharged for beer and hid their women. Eventually, Wolfgang's journey home seemed no more heroic to my youthful eyes than did my maiden voyage abroad.

The Eternal Quest

It was several years before I would seriously study mythology from a spiritual point of view and see Wolfgang's and my journey to Germany in the perspective of the hero's journey, with the various stages of leaving home, meeting challenges and growth, and returning to the village of origin. It was still later, while working with students and clients, that I began to fully understand the lessons that myths have to tell us all—that life as a journey is a central archetype in human consciousness and a central element for healing our rift with God. It is part of our "hard-wire," the way our souls organize our development and keep us continually progressing and evolving in the way that's right for us, from business life or motherhood in one stage to seeking God in the next.

In each stage of life, as we encounter obstacles to our growth, we participate in this archetypal pattern of the Quest. Wolfgang and I were in different stages of our journeys, but we were following the same archetypal pattern on our paths to becoming adult men. These "growing up to adulthood" stages have to happen before we get to the more consciously followed spiritual paths we travel today. If we do not complete a stage, we remain stuck there to some degree or another, which creates a rift.

We carry an image of the next stage we are to navigate in our unconscious parts—actual feelings and images that guide us on our way. I remember that imaging and feeling while a boy on the farm, imagining as I threw rocks against the barn that I were Ted Kluzuski, my favorite baseball player. At other times I was John Wayne, saving the farm during the cattle wars. And as I was out in the fields playing out this archetypal pattern to male wholeness, my sister was in her bedroom curling her hair and dreaming of her feminine quest—conquering her foes on the dance floor, Belle of the Ball, Queen of the May.

This deep inner pattern for growth is common to all humans. It is the urge that moves us through the stages of life, facing our fears of change and the challenges that help us grow and evolve. The Quest takes on different slants and appearances—whether we're going to our first dance or opening our own business—but the urge and the pattern are the same. On shipboard, Wolfgang was returning home for his next lesson in growth—not, of course, what he expected—and I was taking my first journey. But we were both dancing the same waltz. We were becoming ourselves, at our respective stages.

Most of us are close to or beyond mid-life by the time the Quest becomes an obviously spiritual one. We could argue, of course, that all paths and journeys are spiritual, in that they lead us to evolve in appropriate ways for the various stages of life. But the spiritual path is qualitatively different, in that it is an *internal* journey, while the ones prior to it were more oriented to the external world. My quests to make the basketball team in high school, join the army, go to college, and get married were externally referenced journeys, accompanied by the usual hope that they would be *the answer* and I would live happily ever after. But my spiritual awakening in Utah and after has been a wholly internal affair. I have given up the idea that something out there is *the answer*. Whatever else I have done or accomplished since my awakening has been the result of my inner life, the will and the work of God.

The Journey Inward

When we arrive at the time of our spiritual journey, our path becomes an inward one, while operating on the same hard-wired program described in the great myths. Ulysses is drawn to the Sirens' song. Buddha sits under the bodhi tree. In my work as a spiritual teacher and holistic counselor, I consider that my clients and students are on a hero's journey to health, well-being, and wholeness. In offering them this context for their search, I am giving them a container in which to receive healing support from the universe. Mythologist Joseph Campbell said that "myth is the aperture through which the energies of the universe pour into human history." When people show up at my meditation class, or for counseling and bodywork, I tell them to congratulate themselves for beginning the journey inward. It is a very important step in life, for by turning inward, we have to some degree or another graduated beyond some of our outward projections.

At this point in our lives we have recognized that the answers to our search for health, happiness, and fulfillment are within rather than without, and we are willing to spend time, money, and energy on our *inner quest*—the quest to heal our rift. This inward journey is, of course, governed by the same archetypal pattern as our outward journeys, but the outcome is not limited to stages of life or accomplishment of goals. The journey inward is infinite. It is like peeling the proverbial onion, in that we find layers upon tearful layers until we encounter the core of our beings. And that core is both infinite and divine.

When we encounter the divine core and begin to live there, we discover the vastly improved quality of life it offers. Never in my years of work has it failed to bring the seeker in question a far greater ability to live life fully, to accept life more graciously, and to express more joyfully and creatively in the world. It still amazes me to watch life unfold, ever more abundantly and productively, without the struggling and striving of the outwardly referenced life.

But I get ahead of myself. Living the healed life is the last stage of the spiritual journey, and by far the longest. Like the other heroes' journeys, spiritual healing follows a "blueprint to wholeness," which exists in our consciousness. The myths are in effect our stories, reflected in the mirror of our own consciousness. Once we begin our spiritual journey, what happens for us is not wholly unlike what happened to Buddha, St. Francis, or Gilgamesh—we seek, we struggle, we transcend.

As knowledge of discernible stages of dying has proven helpful to millions of dying people and their families, awareness of the *stages of healing* can be helpful to those of us on the journey of healing our rift with God. Both are models for transformation: we understand the archetype, read others' stories, and do as they've done.

THE STAGES OF HEALING

I have found little difference between the recovery stories of my clients and students and the myths of antiquity. The stages of healing, especially, all seem about the same. Josie, the secretary with a drinking problem, is just as heroic when she gets sober, finds God and herself at AA, and goes back to her family as was Hamlet the Prince of Denmark when he sailed back from England to restore his kingdom—with the basic difference, of course, that Josie finds God and gets to live a lot longer than Hamlet.

The five stages of healing I have identified are *awareness of suffering*, *searching for the magic fix*, *the bottom—when fixing fails*, *awakening to our inner authority*, and *living the healed life*. When Josie the secretary realizes she has a drinking problem, she is at stage one, aware of the suffering that alcoholism causes; when she tries to solve her problem by drinking only wine with dinner, she is trying the easy answers at the stage of the magic fix; at stage three, Josie hits her bottom by getting drunk again and getting a drunken-driving ticket; she moves to stage four and the inner authority by seeking counseling, joining AA, and turning her life over to God; and in the final stage, Josie lives the healed life for many years, continuing to grow spiritually, dealing with the underlying issues of her drinking problem, and encouraging others to embark on their own healing journeys.

I might add that the first three stages of healing are usually the easiest to complete, and the last one is the hardest. Becoming aware of our suffering may happen of its own accord, and we may easily go in search of the magic fix and hit a very deep bottom. But it requires something extraordinary for us to withdraw our attention from the kaleidoscopic attractions in the world of work, sex, and gurus long enough to find our own inner authority; it requires even more personal will and power to bring it all back to the village and live the healed life. Even a little dab of healing the rift is helpful, of course. We can take just one step at a time and let the momentum of the journey carry us home to Self.

AWARENESS OF SUFFERING

I believe we are all one living being, connected at the heart, and when Gautama Buddha discovered suffering people, he discovered his own suffering. The Buddhist path, therefore, is all about how the individual may relieve this suffering and find happiness, as are perhaps all paths. What Buddha and all true spiritual teachers find is that until we become our true selves and heal our rifts with God, we suffer greatly. But because we have always suffered, we are like the person who has a rock in her shoe and has so adjusted to it that she is not aware of the pain it gives her. Until we become aware of our suffering, we cannot stop it.

Mabel did not believe that she suffered when she first came to our basic meditation class. She was simply experiencing hypertension "from having so much fun" and wanted to calm down a bit. Besides, her friend Fred was taking the course and she thought it would "be a kick to learn how to zombie out."

I have never seen anyone who was in as much pain as Mabel was resist the awareness of it as much as she did. Awareness is the essence of what we teach meditators: awareness of bodily sensations, awareness of breath, awareness of emotions, and awareness of thoughts. Keep at it and you might become aware of yourself as God. But first you must become aware of yourself. Mabel wanted to learn to meditate but she didn't want to become aware of herself, let alone God. She was in too much pain to even consider facing it.

"What if you don't want to know all that stuff?" she asked. "I'm having a good time in my life. Why would I want to find out that I'm unhappy and in pain? What good will that do?"

Mabel asked hard questions. "Do you hear what you're saying, Mabel?" my co-teacher, Jim Charlton, asked. "You're saying you'd rather live the lie that you're happy than face the possible truth that you're in pain and faking it. Nothing can change that way. Is that what you really want?"

"Why not?" Mabel asked. "If I'm happy in my ignorance, why should I admit I'm unhappy and be miserable? What's the payoff here?"

I loved Mabel. She confused most of the other class members in the process, but she would not budge until she got a suitable answer. "You'll have to trust us on this one, Mabel," I said. "You don't have to meditate, and we won't blame you if you don't. It's clearly your choice. But if you stick with it, you'll gradually find a track that will take you through whatever suffering you discover right to the other side. You will never regret the journey, I promise."

Many people with deep spiritual wounds are like Mabel, in the beginning. They are drawn to solve a "little problem" they do not deem painful. They do not want to know about the great suffering beneath the surface, of which their "little problem" is only a symptom. Mabel was not unusual in her avoidance of awareness, but she *was* unusual in the amount of pain she was hiding, and she was unusually clear about her avoidance of it. Most of us unenlightened people are resistant to awareness. We are trapped—as the masters tell us—in ignorance of ourselves, in illusion. We humans have a dual nature. In our cosmic state we are God fully aware of Himself, omniscient and omnipotent, one with all. In our dualistic state we are individual egos, unaware of our divine nature, as caught in the drama of our daily existence as flies on flypaper.

In our egocentric state, we are so lost in our ignorance that we have no idea who we are. Nearly 100 percent of the beginners who come to my classes and office are out of touch with their emotions, bodily feelings, intuition, and thought patterns. At the beginner's stage of awareness, we identify with our egocentric conditioning. We are strangers to ourselves. And the worst of it is that we are *unaware* that we are unaware. When asked if we are aware of body and emotions, we will generally say yes. And the more unaware we are, the more vehement the "yes." When we're the most in pain, we're often the least aware of our wounds. That's the nature of such wounds—they hurt so much we have to push them away for protection.

Most people seeking meditation instruction or counseling for the first time, therefore, have no idea what they are in for. A few have started the awareness-of-suffering stage but haven't traveled far. Beginning meditation students want a little "something," "a taste of what Deepak Chopra is talking about," or what Mabel called "a little trick to play on my blood pressure." Those seeking counseling want "a minor adjustment in my relationships" or "your opinion about what I should do." We have no idea that a little awareness goes a long, long way.

When someone walks into my office or classes with that "little trick" attitude, I often feel like a dishwasher being handed a tiny plate to wash while the person unknowingly conceals a huge pile of dirty dishes from both herself and me. I know how it is. I have done the same with my counselors. I have been the one handing one tiny saucer to my teacher, half knowing about the stack of dirty dishes piling up in my sink. The image is similar to that of the huge sack of shadow material Robert Bly describes: everyone but us can see the black sack we're dragging along behind. But in spite of ourselves, life seems to turn us around, to make us aware of all those crusted-over dishes of our suffering. Until then, all we want washed is that tiny plate we offer so tentatively, because we don't want anything changed in what we'd like to believe is our tidy little universe.

As Mabel continued to meditate, she became one of our superstars. As she watched her body and emotions, she became aware of her pattern of pleasing others in order to feel all right about herself. Later on, as she swept beyond the "magic fix" stage and hit bottom, she became aware of feeling deeply inadequate, afraid, and insecure. She realized she had run from these feelings all of her life through overachievement, promiscuity, excessive exercise to stay attractive to men, and heavy drinking. Yet in spite of all her efforts to keep herself "up," she experienced a deep emptiness and loneliness she felt incapable of filling.

"At that point, I wanted to run like hell," she later reported, "but there was no place to go. I couldn't lie to myself anymore. 'Damn,' I said to myself. 'Here you are at fifty-eight; your body's in pain and falling apart from all that booze and exercise, and now you're wise to all your old scams. What have you got us into now?'"

Mabel stuck with her program and gradually came out the other side. Through a combination of meditation, spiritual-group work, and counseling, she became fully aware of the intense suffering that had long been present in her life, about which she had been completely ignorant, and she learned to embrace and transcend it. The total blueprint for this recovery process is right there in our consciousness, and we are sure to find it if we become as dedicated and sincere as Mabel.

The Ton of Cabbage

A Sufi story told by Idries Shah about a ton of cabbage puts awareness in perspective: A society of people were dispossessed of their homeland, a paradise that only a few people remembered. Those few were expert swimmers who could teach others to swim back to this paradise, an island some miles away. But knowledge of this ancestral home was forbidden in the regime, so only a few knew about it, and even fewer dared to seek out these few for swimming instruction. Still worse, when even those few seekers arrived for instruction, they came with a ton of cabbage on their backs, because they knew it was a long trip and they couldn't see how they could survive without it. Imagine the job of those swimmers to teach their new students, first, that they had a ton of cabbage on their backs, and second, that they would have to dump their load of cabbage if they expected to swim to the promised land. Some would say that even the Hebrew prophet Moses couldn't let go of enough of his personal cabbage to get across the river Jordan.

The cabbage is the stuff of our conditioned minds, of course, that which causes our suffering. And it is fear that inhibits our awareness of it. Our egos have been busy inhibiting our awareness from the beginning. It took me over thirty years and a spiritual breakdown to face the personal cabbage of my childhood pain, which I had carried with me all along, unaware. It is part of our survival instinct to push from consciousness that which we are not able to handle at the moment. But survival has its price. We limit so much of ourselves from awareness that we lose our own souls. We create gaping rifts with God.

Our shame and our fears of inadequacy and worthlessness also keep us in denial. In the West we are taught to shun emotional people who "make a big deal out of things." If we acknowledged their pain, we would be tacitly approving of their openly expressing it. And that would be far too threatening to those of us who strive to ignore our own pain. So we act "normal," pretend no one else is suffering, and keep our own suffering a secret from everyone, including ourselves. What we don't know is that love and healing cannot enter a closed, dark container and that becoming aware of our pain and revealing it to ourselves and others is the first step to healing. What is hidden cannot be helped. Awareness of suffering brings the vast possibility of spiritual recovery.

SEARCHING FOR THE MAGIC FIX

Hardly any of us fails to try the magic-fix stage on our journey to healing. Once we become aware of our suffering, our first impulse is to fix it—by any means we can find. And today, as always, there are many magic bullets and magic wands available for us to try.

And why shouldn't we? Most of us have worked hard to establish our power base, or at least a little bit of security. When something happens to our bodies or emotions, we want to "fix" it as soon and as easily as possible and get on with living our lives as they were. Few of us are like the sage who got hit by the brick in the story in chapter 2. We don't stop to ponder what happened to us and why. We want to get fixed, not changed.

Accidents, illnesses, divorces, or the simple awareness of suffering signify change in the status quo, which is threatening to most of us. The recidivism rate for released convicts is phenomenal. They have been known to walk down the street from prison, rob a store, and wait for the police, just to get back into a world they know and in which they are comfortable. People in abusive relationships often experience the same fear. Often reared by abusive parents, they know fear very well. Anything else is the dark woods, the threatening unknown that must be crossed through on the hero's journey.

Russell's Butter Dial

I met Russell back in the days when hypnosis was one of my primary tools for helping people to wholeness. Hypnotherapy attracts a great number of people in the magic-fix stage because of its reputation as a tool in magic: "If it can make people believe they're dogs and bark on national television, it ought to be able to fix me." The Magic Fixer, remember, is bent on removing what he perceives to be "the problem," but he doesn't want to change anything. Perception is the main obstacle to those in the magic-fix stage, because we can't yet "see" that we need to pass through the dark woods and change something in ourselves in order to be healed. Like the magician who pulls a tablecloth out from under the carefully set dishes, we hope to remove the soiled part of us without disturbing the rest.

Russell, a big, dark-complexioned macho man of thirty-four, wanted a fix on his sexual issue. "Look," he said, being as blunt and direct as a football coach describing the big play, "I don't want a whole lot of psychobabble stuff here. I'm just having a little problem with erections. It's no big deal. I've been a real stud most of my life. Had broads all over me and I didn't care about any of them. I could do two or three a night. But now I've met Belinda, the one woman I want, and everything has gone wrong. It's terrible." Suddenly he shifted and moved back farther into his chair, stifling his obviously painful emotions before they could get out of control.

"I don't want to talk about it, man. Just fix it."

"Uh, Russell, could we talk about this a *little* more?" I asked, feeling that I was not being handed even the token single dish from the pile he so closely guarded. Russell was obviously as lopsided as a man can get in his sexual attitudes and behavior. But he wasn't about to open that subject.

"No," he said firmly. "I don't want to talk about it. Talking only makes me think about it, and when I think about it I get scared and it all gets too real. This is *not* real," he said with emphasis. "What's real is I'm a stud. So I don't want to talk about it."

Russell was a very big man and quite commanding. If I'd had a magic wand around then—as perhaps Viagra is today—I'm sure I would have waved it for him, just as I might throw hamburger to a big snarling dog. But I didn't have a wand. So I asked him what he had in mind, hoping to find an opening for a dash to the pile of dishes behind him.

"Well, I was watching that lady hypnotist on TV, Pat something, and when I got up to get a beer I got this idea." He became visibly excited as he leaned forward to explain. "I saw the dial on the butter drawer in the refrigerator. You can set it for 'hard' or you can set it for 'soft.'" Russell stood up and paced as he laid out his touchdown strategy: "So I want you to hypnotize me to believe I got that dial on my chest, see, 'hard' or 'soft.' Get it? Then all I gotta do when I close my eyes and kiss Belinda is see the dial turn to 'on' and get with the program. Can you do that?" Then, as if he had shown too much vulnerability and needed to let me know he was still in charge, he added, "Or I'll have to find somebody who can."

I'm a man, and I felt Russell's pain very deeply. Here was a man with a dangerously one-sided attitude whose emotions and body were calling him back into balance. At thirty-four it was time for him to grow out of his "high school football star" attitude about women and life. It was time to deal with feelings. Like everything in the universe, his suffering had a reason for being there. As Einstein said, "God does not play dice with the universe." Russell's suffering was bringing his awareness to his emotions and sexuality and subsequently to his relationship with women and life. Change was in the air for Russell, and he wanted no part of it.

Avoiding Change in the Magic-Fix Stage

Few of us volunteer for change. We usually wait until we're kicked into it. Though Russell was hardly fully aware of his suffering—which would take him into the pain that he so aggressively avoided—his macho image was sufficiently tattered that he jumped squarely into the search for the magic fix. Russell is not greatly different from the rest of us. Few of us like change, though we may think we do. When a flu comes on us, we want antibiotics to kick it fast. We don't want to ask what it's about and what it has to say to us.

Chinese medicine, for example, tells us that if we are *aware* some three days before a cold or flu hits, we might notice a tiredness and lack of energy. And if we listen to that tiredness and go straight to bed, we can often avoid getting sick. But that would call for a change in lifestyle and attitude, wouldn't it? We would much rather have a cafe mocha and kick our tired bodies back on the track to work and fun.

Once again, a rift with Self is another version of a rift with God. A neurosis, for example, has been called "an attempt at self-cure." From a spiritual perspective, all physical and emotional suffering is a call for attention to what is out of balance and unacknowledged. We have something to learn that has the potential for transforming our lives, opening to our greater potential, becoming more fully ourselves—and healing our rift with God. And that's scary.

Nelson Mandela, in his inaugural speech in 1994, said, "Our deepest fear is not that we are inadequate. Our deepest fear is that we are powerful beyond measure. It is our light, not our darkness, that frightens us." The search for the magic fix is about that fear of our own power, our surrender to the only power in the universe. Our fear is about releasing the old and outworn and embracing the God-self of our true nature. So we frantically try to fix the old. And it's all OK. It's a natural human process toward that larger goal of healing our rift with God. "All roads lead to heaven," the Chinese proverb says.

But often the fixing works. The cancer is sliced away, hypnosis works, the marriage is saved. What then? Often, true healing stops. We return to our old lives untouched by change. If our problem had any message for us, prescribed any adjustment for our lives, we didn't hear it. We stop our healing at the second stage. Why does the process halt with the quick fix? Because we failed to reach *the bottom—the real messenger of change*. Most of us will not stop and listen to the messenger unless she knocks us down, sits on our chest, and pulls our hair. We don't give in unless we have to. Only another major crisis, something big enough to wake us up, will move us out of the magic fix and on to the next stage.

THE BOTTOM—WHEN FIXING FAILS

Russell tried several fixes before hitting bottom. Most of us do. It's part of process. Only if and when the fixing fails do we fall into the pit that we've avoided all along—and hit bottom. If we get fixed with no growth involved—the way most of us would like it—we avoid hitting bottom for the present, but we might need another whack at a later date and time as the organism continues its efforts to self-heal. And the next whack might just prove to be a little harder, a little more painful! For example, physicians have found that suppressing the symptoms of eczema may cause it to reappear as asthma, a debilitating and sometimes fatal illness.

On the other hand, if we get fixed and grow even a little bit in the process, we can possibly avoid the bottom. If we grow just enough to inch our old dysfunctional foundation back under us, we may go on functioning that way for years. It is said that democracy survives like that, changing a little bit when it has to. A complete revolution isn't always necessary. But hopefully we will grow enough through our suffering to acquire a more flexible way of being in the world and get on with the hero's journey in some capacity or another. If we do, we will flow with change when the next storm hits.

It's when we stubbornly persevere in imposing our egocentric will at all costs—demanding that the world conform to our outdated concepts of it, no quarter given—and still don't get fixed that we hit bottom. Nature isn't cruel with her symptoms; it's our *own* imbalance and one-sidedness that get us in trouble. All of our demanding and struggling has made no difference. Every machination and strategy has only dug the hole deeper until we finally despair of ever getting out. When every other effort has failed, we finally give up the ego ghost and surrender.

Mabel hit that bottom after practicing meditative awareness for a while. As the months went by, she became more and more aware of the suffering she had ignored for so long, and she had no solution for fixing it. Like Russell, she was a powerful mover-and-shaker who'd had her way with life. She didn't know what to do with feelings and vulnerability any more than he. To let go of control and experience their feelings is terribly frightening for people like Mabel and Russell. "What's going to happen? Who'll hold it all together? What will happen to me?" they ask—all very good questions.

In the bottom stage, the all-powerful ego gets its comeuppance. The bottom feels like a bad thing—a very bad thing. And most of our friends agree, because they, too, look at the world through egocentric eyes. Ever since childhood, the ego has been running the show, sure that it knows what is right for the entire organism and holding everything in place with a tight rein. Though it has only a minuscule view of reality, it believes that it sees and knows everything, and it strives desperately to control everything and everybody within its range of influence. So for just about everybody, the bottom looks like the wrong place to be.

To give due credit, the ego does a fine job of helping us survive. And without the survival instinct, we probably wouldn't have made it to this stage of life. But life is not *only* about survival—it is also about growing and becoming far more than the ego can conceptualize. It can only understand growth in the egocentric sense of money, power, and status. Faulty and limited perception is the ego's downfall, for in order to exercise its power, the ego has divorced itself from God and nature, locking instincts and intuitions, feelings and emotions into the prison of unconsciousness, declaring its own petty authority as the one and only. It has made us one-sided and unbalanced. As with all petty tyrants, this one has to fall for the greater good.

In truth, we are spiritual beings in human form. We seem to need strong egos to survive. But in our bottom times—when our egos cannot save us with outdated plans and machinations—we become aware of a greater authority in the castle. We begin to experience our Real Self, our Inner Authority, and with it a trust that our instincts and intuitions will guide us to places where our egos fear to tread.

"Fools rush in where wise men fear to go," says the old song. The "fool" within us is the crazy wisdom of our soul. We begin to understand that we are actually on solid ground when the ego lets go. Something is there to take over, and it knows what's happening and how to handle things. We realize a new, flexible way of living life that allows us to be calm and peaceful and to trust the process of life as it unfolds. We learn to grow fond of this bottom in which we've landed.

Dredging "the Bottom" in Search of Self

All bottoms *look* the same, but like fingerprints, no two bottoms are alike. When I hit mine in Utah, I felt like I was hanging on to life by a raveled thread, my ego so shattered and raw I no longer had control of my emotions and instincts. Unconscious contents poured forth at will, and my ego's frail efforts to contain them were fruitless. It was frightening, and it was fantastic! Pulling to the roadside during panic attacks,

I would play with the border between ego control and chaos, telling the unconscious, "Have your way with me while I meditate, because once I open my eyes I will go on about my business." At other times I would stand on a rock in the midst of a rushing mountain stream for eternities, letting what seemed like infinity flow around me like planets round the stars until I found my proper orbit in the universe— my Self, God.

That's what also happened to Mabel and Russell and millions like us. The harder the head, the bigger the bottom. Alcoholics Anonymous popularized the term *the bottom* and defined how to work with it. Hitting the bottom is a good thing no matter how it feels, they point out. The ego's schemes for redemption fail and fall, making room for God. Once that happens, one is able to recognize a Higher Power and to turn one's life over to it. Folks in "the program" quickly learn to avoid rescuing their brothers and sisters on a bottom. Rescuing them robs them of the powerful learning a bottom has to offer. Instead, they learn to listen and support without "enabling"—without doing it for them. Strength and power are gained through a properly handled bottom.

Holistic health professionals also have the problem of when to intervene and when not. With the advent of our new friends Prozac and Zoloft, the decision is even harder. Is psychopharmacology part of the magic fix? How do we differentiate between a genuine psychological breakdown and a bottom? These are tough questions to which I don't pretend to know the answers. The emotional symptoms of the two experiences are often similar, though physical symptoms may vary. Many doctors, quite unaware of spiritual transformation because of their rational-material orientation, dispense the new drugs more enthusiastically than they once handed out Valium. They don't ask these questions because they don't acknowledge spiritual growth and don't know about bottoms.

Some spiritual directors, however, and some of the new transpersonal, or spiritual, psychologists—because they have hit bottom and are healing their own rifts with God—are able to ask these questions of themselves and their clients. They know that a bottom is often a part of that process. If I were to experience another bottom,

I would want a guide who asked these questions. Some Eastern teachers know *the bottom*—along with its physical and emotional symptoms—as the kundalini experience, an awakening and evolution of spiritual forces—and treat it with the reverence of an honored guest.

My unconscious once told me in a dream how to work with someone at the bottom: "It's OK to help, but don't interfere." I understood: "Be there. Be supportive. Ask the right questions. Don't do it for them." When we try to help others by fixing, by taking the pain away at all costs, we may become part of the problem; we become the narcotic which enables them to hold on to the addictive fantasies that keep them trapped. Like a woman in labor, the bottom dweller needs to know that anesthesia is available, but it is her choice whether or not to use it. A natural phenomenon of birth, like physical pregnancy, a bottom is in my opinion hard-wired into our systems as a fail-safe mechanism to keep stubborn people like me from a lifetime of slavery to the ego. It literally forces us to be born, to turn to our Inner Authority, the God within. There's no place else to go.

Some of my students and clients have asked if they absolutely *need* to have a painful bottom in order to find God. Not at all. Not everyone is as stuck and stubborn as many of us can be. Some folks I know have what I've heard called "seamless bottoms," transitions to the Inner Authority that are hardly noticeable. How nice for them! It doesn't have to be painful. But on the other hand, it's important to note that some folks *think* they have crossed into the Promised Land while they are still wandering in the desert, far from the river Jordan. This is an area where a trusted guide can be helpful. Those who have crossed over the river can usually recognize others who have also done so. If one has not surrendered the ego to God, she has not yet crossed the river.

There's an old story about letting go and its terrors. A drunk man named Jonah had been stumbling his way home along a cliff above the sea when he suddenly slipped off the cliff. He grabbed a frail branch about halfway down the cliff to momentarily save himself from the otherwise terminal fall on the rocks a hundred feet below. Terrified, he hung on to the branch with all of his drunken strength, but he knew he couldn't last long. To his surprise, he heard himself praying: "Oh, God, I know we never talk, and I'm sorry. But if you save my butt this time, I'll be much better. I'll quit drinking, stay home with my wife and kids—anything. Just tell me what to do."

Glancing upward, Jonah saw that the darkness had vanished from the sky above him, and a pure white light shone straight through the darkness, illuminating the cliff and the branch to which he was so frantically holding.

It was then that he heard a voice: "Let go of the branch, Jonah." The voice was at once powerful and gentle. But he must be mistaken. Looking down at the rocks, he knew he must have heard wrong.

"What did you say, Lord? I thought I heard you, but that could not be right. I want you to save me, Lord. So tell me what to do."

"Trust thou me, Jonah. To be saved by me, let go of the branch." The powerful voice boomed through the darkness, unmistakable even above the ocean's roar.

Jonah paused, his hand tighter than ever on the branch, and he glanced down again at what his every sense told him was sure death. But God had spoken. What to do? Finally an idea flashed across his face and he shouted back into the light: "Ah, just checking, but is there anyone *else* up there I could talk to?"

We have no word on whether Jonah let go of the branch or not. Like most of us in his position, however, he had little choice. To hang on to the branch and demand another God would have been like trying to negotiate with an H-bomb—there is no choice but unconditional surrender. When we hit bottom, we have to let go and trust. Everything else has failed. There's nowhere to go for help and nothing to do. We have to let go.

The good news is that when we let go, God catches us. The moment we let go of the ego's dualistic ignorance, we are released into the universe of unlimited possibilities of which our ego minds know nothing. We humble beings are awash in a universal soup of intelligent energy consciousness that is responsive to us. When Nobel Prize–winner John Addington studied the universe of order within the matrix of subatomic particles, he described it as the "mind of God." And so it is. The universe is responsive to our beliefs and thoughts about ourselves and it.

While our old egocentric way of living was through fear and control, our new way after the bottom will be through faith, trust, intention, compassion, and unconditional love. We don't know this when we're on our bottom. Only when we fully let go and find out that a safety net was there all the time, holding us up when we thought we were doing it ourselves, do we see the true nature of reality. We find that we were like children playing in a park, thinking we're all alone, while all along there were trustworthy adults watching after us— parents, teachers, and guardians of all sorts. We were taken care of and protected all along, and we didn't know it.

Awakening to Our Inner Authority

How wonderful it is to walk out of the Valley of the Shadow of Death that is the bottom and walk into the sunshine of the Inner Authority. How truly sweet it is, for in the bottom we let go, we surrender. We stop clinging to the branch, and we are caught in the arms of God. As the 23rd Psalm of David says, "I will fear no evil: for thou art with me; thy rod and thy staff they comfort me." The only way most of us can know that we are "safe" is by surrendering our egocentric dominance in the bottom stage and experiencing being caught in God's arms as we awaken to our Inner Authority.

Learning to Bow to the "Wise Sergeant" Within

The insecure ego, afraid to let go of control, reminds me of some green lieutenants I met in the army. Now, the armed services are run by sergeants. Don't let anyone tell you differently. Every unit has a sergeant in charge. It also has a lieutenant who may *think* he is in charge because he is of higher rank. But while the lieutenant has just entered the army and has only a year or two of *theoretical* experience, the sergeant has been around for over a decade and knows how things *really* work. He knows how to read the maps, talk to the locals, acquire needed information and equipment, get the best from his men and women, and run the outfit efficiently.

Now, if a new lieutenant is wise, he knows that fact and will defer his authority until he learns what the sergeant can teach him. Gradually they form a working relationship that benefits them both as well as their platoon members and the army.

But if the lieutenant is unwise and insecure, he will reject the sergeant's willing assistance and immediately assert himself as the authority. Within days, as the whole company watches with amusement, he will make a fool of himself, completely helpless to control the multitude of intricate details that make a unit work effectively. Like an errant child who must give in to mother, the lieutenant is forced to surrender to his sergeant's superior wisdom in order for balance to return again.

The same thing is true for the bottom most of us will confront. There is an intelligence within ourselves and the universe that is ancient beyond measure. It has been operating before the beginning of time and will be forever. It is the force that moves the universe around its core, that operates the tides and the evolution of life, and that keeps our entire natural system unfolding on schedule in balance and harmony.

The ancient master Lao Tzu called it Tao, the Way. It is in all of nature, and it is in us humans as a part of nature. It is our eternal sergeant who knows intuitively and instinctively how to get the job done—easily and naturally, without worry and fear. It is the Holy Spirit of Christianity, the ki of Japan, the prana of India. It understands synchronicity—the way a multitude of people, events, and circumstances interrelate for universal good. It knows that when you or I pay attention to the nature of things and form a firm intention about what is good for us, the Tao responds to give it to us. But that intention will not come from the green lieutenant, the ignorant ego who does not yet know the nature of things. It will come from the wise sergeant who is humble and who knows how things really work in the universe.

When we hit bottom and awaken to the Inner Authority, we're encountering the wise sergeant within ourselves and the universe and turning the platoon over to Him or Her. Like the maturing lieutenant, we watch and learn, letting the sergeant run things, intervening only to ask questions or talk over decisions. After all, the lieutenant is important, also. When he is functioning in an enlightened manner, he has something to offer. His job in the chain of command is to stay attuned to both the sergeant and God in the world, observing synchronicity, asking the right questions, and letting the sergeant know about his concerns. When he becomes wise, he will again assume authority in the tasks of the world—but humbly—for the wise acknowledge their own helplessness and ignorance and bow willingly to the Inner Authority.

The Way of the Inner Authority Is That of "Least Effort"

This way of living is known in Taoism as *wei wu wei*—doing without doing. The master knows Tao well enough to cooperate with it, using "the law of least effort" in order not to overdo and interfere with the Tao. In prayer, it is the way of "calling God's attention" to a situation without presuming to know the ideal outcome: "O Lord or Lady, I ask you to notice the sick child in the next building here who has cancer. And if it's *your will*, I would like to see her cured of it. I see her recovering and growing up to fulfill her potential, if it be your will. Amen."

Despite the ego's fears to the contrary, living is easy when we "let go and let God." Most suffering in life is caused—as our lieutenant learned—by our holding on to control. But when we follow the way of *wei wu wei*, we remain in surrender at all times and thus give up our suffering. But that is living the healed life, a difficult task to say the least, and our next stage in healing our rift with God.

LIVING THE HEALED LIFE

When I left the mountains of Utah, I was in the euphoria of original surrender, and it was magnificent. I realized that I had never before trusted the universe to do its part in the bargain of making my life work. And because I had tried in the past to do too much while knowing too little, I had practically botched the entire experiment. Afterward, as I drove back to California, I was in a totally surrendered state, open to the infinite potentialities that God had always offered me but which I had never before seen.

Unforeseen incidents and synchronous meetings rocketed me along my path at unprecedented speed when I arrived in California. Doors opened and events unfolded as though I were a visiting dignitary whose itinerary has been previously planned and arranged by unknown secretaries and underlings. Arriving in the San Francisco Bay area, I had no idea what I would do other than write. I was simply drawn here by my newly discovered Inner Authority. Within two weeks I was launched in the career as a helper that I continue to this day.

I thought that all there was to it was to get on *Mr. Toad's Wild Ride* and stay on it until my ticket expired. But I was wrong. As the great Indian teacher Paramahansa Yogananda said, "Environment is stronger than will power." It was relatively easy for me to stay inspired and surrendered as long as I was alone, had nothing, and was going nowhere in particular. "When you don't know where you're going, all roads lead there," says an old Jewish proverb. Wandering mendicants have it better than we think, for when we wander, we are pulled by God's grace like iron filings to an invisible magnet.

As time passed, however, and the new life God gave me got complicated with relationships and responsibilities, I slipped and fell. How will all of these tasks get done? Where's the money supposed to come from? The winds of fear and attachment soon brought struggle and worry to sit on my shoulders, and God was blown out the window. Pretty soon I was back being the arrogant lieutenant, attached to outcomes and feeling the burden of one who has to make things happen.

It was then I realized that my journey of healing my rift was far from over; in fact, it had barely begun. My spiritual path was already established for me, and all I had to do was walk it without falling into the underbrush. But that was proving to be a far bigger job than I anticipated. I realized that I needed to stabilize my newfound awakening, so I began surveying churches, temples, and synagogues, searching for an enlightened community of believers that matched what my Inner

Authority had in mind for me. It had to be one with a philosophical ceiling high enough to accept all religions and with a system of training that would help me integrate my awakening and live the healed life. After years of searching, I found all of that and helped create the healing groups I work with today.

Living the healed life is a notoriously difficult task for the newly surrendered initiate. I was reared in a Christian community where becoming "saved" by taking Jesus Christ "for your personal savior" was the principal way of healing the rift. Salvation is a powerful and potentially life-saving experience, and I have witnessed it many times, having been saved and baptized in the Baptist faith when young. I have also witnessed the tragic fall from grace so many Christians subsequently take, many on national television. These falls are an embarrassment to Christians and a source of bitter laughter for people who have felt judged or injured by Christian organizations and converts.

But these "falls from grace" are not limited to Christians. We universalists have also watched well-known teachers of Buddhist, Hindu, Jewish, and Muslim faiths fall. Many of us remember Bhagavan Das, a teacher of Richard Alpert. Alpert's story itself is about healing his rift with God through his trip to India, where American Bhagavan Das—a twenty-three-year-old sadhu, or holy man, loved by the Indian faithful—was a key player in his healing. Alpert eventually returned to America as Ram Dass and became a major spiritual teacher.

Bhagavan Das was another story, however. Sacred as he had become, when he returned to America, he soon left his spiritual sadhana (practices) and, in his words, "lost it completely. I didn't have *satsang*. You must have good company. You have to hang out with pure people, with people who really are on the path, who are sincere, and who elevate your mind."

Bhagavan Das was away from God for over twenty years. "I rejoined the world and lived as a businessman. I sold cars in Santa Cruz . . . then I moved into direct sales. . . . I probably averaged $3,000–$5,000 every month. Fancy suits, expensive cars—I did the whole trip." Finally he encountered another spiritual teacher who brought him back to the path.

"How do you come to be in the presence of God?" he now asks. "By remembering God. Divine thoughts bring you to divinity. Maharaj sent me back to America to inspire people to get their practice going because that's what is going to transform them."

Establishing a Spiritual Practice

What is a "spiritual practice"? It is whatever you do to keep your healing progressing, to keep you as surrendered and open to God as you were in your bottom phase. In my experience, no spiritual path is superior to any other. Christians who are "saved" and baptized are different from Bhagavan Das only in the tradition with which their Inner Authority is attuned, and that is up to God. God's ways are superior to those of our egos. We are drawn by our innards to the God-path of healing and wholeness that is appropriate for us. The only questions worth asking for the recovering person are "How can I keep from losing the connection to God and Self I've found and continue evolving?" and "Is the path I've chosen leading me to a holistically sound healed life?"

Two aspects of spiritual practice that we all must consider are our spiritual company or community and the specific actions we individually take to grow personally and spiritually. Keeping company with like-spirited friends is very important for helping us stay strong and committed to the spiritual path. Sincere and dedicated people support and reinforce our own dedication to the path. I would also recommend that some members of your spiritual company understand holistic health and know as you do that a rift with Self is a rift with God. At the same time, we must be very attentive that the specific actions we take each day help support our spiritual intentions rather than sabotage them. Remember, our old habits have had us in their grasp for many years. We need all the help we can get to slip their grasp and establish a healed life.

Your practice, if you are a yogi, may consist of intense meditation every day. If you are Muslim, you will face Mecca, fall to your knees, and pray five times a day. If you are Christian, you may pray constantly, read the Bible, or help others less fortunate than you. If you are a Buddhist, you may practice mindfulness. Whatever your faith, you may talk constantly to God, asking for guidance. You may fast, bathe in holy water, take pilgrimages to holy places, give all your goods to the poor— the possibilities are endless. But whatever your practice, it must be a consistent, daily experience, and it must take you beyond thought and ego into the Land of God. Otherwise it is not doing its job.

I once heard a famous author and teacher tell of coming back from his life as a monk and gradually "losing it." Like most of us, he had to make a living. That prompted his return into the web of his old ways, and he was soon shocked to find himself back in his previous marijuana habit. And Dave, a man in my own circle, was "saved" in his youth from a life of alcohol and drug abuse as a rock-band member. He entered a monastery and for fifteen years was an ideal, clean-and-sober monk. Soon after returning to the world, however, he was back on drugs and alcohol, surfing the dens of rock-and-roll as if he had never left.

Dave's experience points again to the need for attention to the whole being. Living the healed life requires that we not use the spiritual path as a means of escaping ourselves but as a means of *finding* ourselves. This is a hero's journey that requires us to "know the Truth," which will set us free. There are many desperate souls who will use the spiritual life as a place to "hide out." Each of us must examine ourselves carefully, remembering the adage that "a life uninvestigated is not worth living."

Like many before me, I thought the bottom was as hard as it gets and the rest would be easy. Not at all. Living the healed life, I must confess, is the hardest thing I've ever done. I like to ask my own students by way of teaching, "Do you know what the really powerful mystics do when they've perfected their practice? They get married, get a job, and live an ordinary life like you and me. That's where the *real path* begins."

The way to be in the presence of God is to remember God as often as possible. There are a thousand ways of doing that. I find it helpful to ask myself where God is "right now," as often as I think of it. That very question brings me into the presence of God, who is always with us, as us. I have also found it helpful—even mandatory—to have a company of spiritual friends, because "Environment is stronger than will power." With their support, my daily practice of prayer, meditation, chanting and singing, spiritual service, and teaching what I know to other willing seekers takes on a strength and power that I could not find alone. All of these are ways to keep us on the path of surrender, following the divine impulse. If we but intend to live the healed life, our Inner Authority will help us find a way to do the rest.

Living the healed life is the last stage on our hero's journey to wholeness. Performing even one or two of the practices recommended here will help immeasurably. To employ the five stages to healing, simply read them over again and find where you are on the journey. Most of us have some awareness of our suffering, have tried a few magic bullets, and have hit at least a mini-bottom or two. We can testify to the power of these stages. But how well do you understand your Inner Authority and living the healed life? These are the stages that people find most elusive on this epic journey. Read on. The next two chapters will help you unlock the remainder of the doors to healing your rift with God.

5

GUIDELINES ON THE PATH TO SPIRITUAL RECOVERY

Helen, whom you met in chapter 3 as a recently divorced recovering religionist in my weight-loss group, arrived at my office with a quizzical look on her face. When I asked her about that look, she immediately released a torrent of questions.

"What now?" she asked. "I understand more about why I got so depressed and fat after the divorce. You were all right about me. I did have a childish view of religion and I got deeply hurt by my church. I felt so *betrayed*!

"But what now? I'm still a Catholic. But not a Catholic in the old sense. I'm neither this nor that. You got me into this with that damned class. What do I do now?"

Helen squirmed in her chair and peered at me with the same innocence that had touched me so deeply in our group. She was still a true believer. Always had been. Always would be. And I knew, having thrown off the authority of the church, she was now looking for someone—some authority—to replace her old-style Catholicism. The church, as the Russian novelist Dostoevsky said decades ago, uses *miracles*, *mystery*, and *authority* to keep its people on the straight and narrow. They keep the Godhead *outside* of the people so that they require an intermediary to reach Him. But Helen, like so many people who've been soul-wounded, found that her thirst could no longer be quenched solely by spiritual water that must first pass through the lips of spiritual authorities. Through our work, she had begun to drink from the sacred spring that flows from the soul of each of us, and she was thirsty for more. Helen was clear about that, but her everyday mind told her she had to find someone else to tell her what to believe.

Therefore, as I acknowledged her fear and urgency, I knew that Helen was in for a big surprise, one she could not yet fathom. She was on course to a profound paradigm shift, one that has become very familiar to me in dealing with my own life and in my work as a holistic health consultant, counselor, bodyworker, and minister. I have found that all core healing is the same, whether it be on a mental, physical, emotional, or spiritual level. As our motto at Integrated Healing Arts states, "All healing is self-healing." It happens not from without but from within, not from the finding of a magic bullet or the right expert authority but from discovering our own *inner authority*. We heal our rift with God just as we heal all wounds—by embarking on an inner journey to one's own Authentic Truth and Identity.

Helen, after much work with her dreams and journaling, found that once she began to understand the inner meaning of the rituals in her church, she could participate more meaningfully and fully. She now feels a deeply satisfying inner connection with God and believes that she has to a great extent healed her rift with God.

Finding the Inner Authority

The good news for Helen and the thousands like her who were spiritually wounded is that they do not have to find some new and exciting religion to replace the old. In fact, such "religion hopping" often causes more wounding. I was pleased that the wise and popular Buddhist teacher Thich Nhat Hahn tells his American audiences that they should not leave their religions and become Buddhists simply because they like some of his teachings. They need to take back the things they learn from other religions and renew their own traditions. Religion hoppers assume—like the lover who jumps from one relationship to another in search of the perfect mate—that their problem is an *outer* one that will be healed when the perfect spiritual group comes along.

Healers have that same problem. Once people realize that Western doctors don't possess godlike powers, they often search for new gods in the alternative health field. We all miss the mark terribly when we search for the answer only outside ourselves, as we all occasionally do. We're fixated by nature on the outer. Remember the old story about God? She hid in the one place that she knew people would never look—inside each of us.

And yet we know that the answer always lies within. No matter how great the skill of an athlete, every coach knows that if the athlete is not clear on the inside, she will never make her mark. No matter how much we worship a high IQ, we know that raw intelligence makes either a great scientist and thinker or a very smart bum, depending on what's inside them. Further, we may have the best medical technology in the world, but when a life-threatening illness ravages an individual, we know that recovery will depend largely on the inner resources of that person. And when someone crosses my path with a spiritual wound, I know that their recovery depends on how much they are willing to shift their attention from the outer world of phenomena to the inner world of spirit and Self.

I had a dream years ago that consisted of only these words: "Follow the Great God Inman." Only when I shared it with a friend did I understand that it was telling me to follow the God *in man*. Of course! Where else would one look for God? We are made in God's image; we are the sons of God, the spirit of God is within us. Whenever we have a genuine experience of God, it is an inner experience. In all of my years with my own spiritual healing and the healing of others on all levels, I have found one constant truth that has never been contradicted: *The healing journey is an inner journey. We must embark on that path to heal, to find peace, to find meaning and purpose in life, to be genuinely content, and to find God.*

But how do we do this? The five basic guidelines to spiritual recovery in the next section lay out the *inner work* necessary for this task. I offer some tips for the outer search in the fourth guideline,

"Connecting in Relationship and Community." But it is my experience that the outer search will largely take care of itself as you become more aware of your inner guidance. We are always guided to exactly the experiences and resources we need for deepening our relationship with God, because God desires this as much as we do.

THE FIVE BASIC GUIDELINES TO SPIRITUAL RECOVERY

As a member of Integrated Healing Arts and Pathways to Self-Healing, I cannot afford to be sectarian in my spiritual life. We all know of the power and helpfulness of enlightened spiritual traditions, and most of us follow one spiritual path or another. We are Christian, Jew, Buddhist, Hindu, shamanic, and Muslim. Yet as healers who encourage people to discover the value of the spiritual life, we do not foist our own spiritual paths off on anyone. This has been a wonderful experience for us all, because we have been forced to find the common denominators of religious and secular organizations. We've sought elements that may be used by anyone who wishes a greater connection with Self and/or God, whether they belong to a religion or not.

Joanne was very helpful to me in giving form to the following guidelines. A short, red-haired woman of forty-five, she was as fiery as her hair was red. She was determined not to "get involved with anything having to do with religion." A self-proclaimed member of rebels against religion, she wanted to recover from her resentment against God and religion, but she was violently opposed to anything that even hinted of religiosity. Any casual mention of soul or spirit would turn her off in a minute, yet she continued to voice her need to heal her rift with God. She was a challenge, to say the least.

"Well, sure I want to get beyond this anger and get in touch with whatever it is that runs the universe," she said one day. "I remember how wonderful it was when I was a kid and could feel that force and know I was taken care of and loved no matter what people did to me. That was an incredible feeling! But the church ruined that for me.

I don't want anything to do with the dogma they stuffed down my throat. It just makes me mad all over again. But I want you to help me get over this. Show me how to connect with my Self and my Greater Self without the baloney."

Joanne wouldn't let me get away with anything. Every guideline or technique I offered her had to be totally clean of any religious overtones or affiliation or she would toss it back in my face. What a gift she continues to be in this respect as I gather together inner tools to help individuals discover themselves and their Higher Power, whether they belong to a religion or not. I have discovered in the process that God and the Self are not confined behind the walls of religions or limited to names. "I am that I am," said Jehovah, making it clear that we can't restrict the Lord of the Universe. God is infinite and can be found only in the human heart and only by those who are willing to embark on a heroic journey. Everyone takes the outer journey to some extent or another. But far fewer embark on the inner journey to healing the rift.

The five basic guidelines to spiritual recovery are universal guideposts for the hero's journey to God and to wholeness. Directing us inward to our own authority, they may be used by anyone who wishes greater health, self-knowledge, and connection with Self and/or God. The person you find within will be the unique being you always knew you were. And the God you find will be *your* God, with whom you will have a more intimate relationship than you could have ever imagined.

The five basic guidelines to spiritual recovery are *inner awareness and acceptance; exploring our assumptions, beliefs, and stories; finding a spiritual vision; connecting in relationship and community;* and *finding self-responsibility for health and spirit.* Once the journey inward begins, the soul responds. And we soon prove for ourselves the promise of the ages—the assurance that if we get on the path to God we will find a broad and solid road that has been waiting for us all the time. And that road will bring us an ease and grace in life that we have never known but which is our birthright. We will be living the life we were meant to live but could only yearn for.

INNER AWARENESS AND ACCEPTANCE

Ralph looked at me as if I had asked him the square root of 746. He had no idea what I was talking about. He wanted me to help him reduce the stress that his doctor had told him was instrumental in his high blood pressure, allergies, and migraines. How was he to know what emotions he felt, what he really wanted in life, or whether or not he liked his job?

"What does all that have to do with my stress, Paul? You come highly recommended, but I don't want to get involved with all this touchy-feely kinda stuff. Let's just do your mumbo-jumbo and let me get back to work."

I sat back in my seat and took a very deep breath. I understood Ralph very well. He was clearly a rational materialist in deep trouble, but he was going to fight and kick all the way to recovery. I, too, had been reared in a macho environment where real men don't feel, where deep thinking about life was for eggheads and sissies. I knew Ralph well. The only things that drive such people to my office are pain and the threat of death.

"Listen, Ralph," I told him. "I came from the same background as you. Working hard and making a living are very important. Without that the family doesn't survive. I know. But you are really out of balance with life and have come to me to get well, and that's going to require that you learn something about yourself, that you become aware of what your mind, emotions, body, and soul are up to so you can live a long healthy life. Now, let's start answering some of the questions I just posed. What do you feel right now?"

Ralph was an extreme case only in his honesty. Any therapist of body, mind, or spirit who has done her own work will testify that the vast majority of first-time clients are extremely unaware of themselves. They may know current events, the batting average of Ken Griffey, or the winner of the Best Actress award at the Oscars. But they don't know about the grief they carry in their chests. They aren't aware of the voice inside that tells them, "You'll never be good enough. You'll always be a failure." They have no idea that the muscles in their upper back are tense. And they certainly don't know that their souls are crying out for them to turn their awareness back from the outer world of success and achievement to the inner world, which is the only place they will find themselves and heal their rifts with God.

When asked by a disciple whether he was a man or a god, the Buddha is said to have replied, "I am aware," or "awake," according to some translations. Mystics of all traditions understand his words. Humans are by nature asleep to their real selves, unaware that the "I" with which they identify is their false self, which we also call the ego. This false self is the identity we took on when we were forced to adopt a certain role in the world. It is the conditioned identity we grew up with. As a farm boy I saw myself as shy and inadequate, rather stupid, rather ugly, and always needing to prove that I was worthwhile and OK, because *I knew that I was not*. I identified closely with that false self. Although I would not have used those exact words to describe myself when I was a young boy, I know that back then I believed every bit of it. That's who I was conditioned to believe was me.

Awareness—A Fundamental Tool

Awareness is a fundamental tool for healing the rift. The mind with its habitual patterns must be trained before we can grasp deep truth. Awareness training begins with the understanding that the conditioned self is not our true identity. And by learning to watch ourselves—the thoughts, feelings, attitudes, beliefs, and actions that are all too automatic—we can gradually begin to see who we actually are. I like to think of the false self as a spacesuit that we crawled into during our formative years. It no longer fits us, and never really did. Yet it controls us, turning us into a sort of robot that's fully programmed to carry out a life of survival on Planet Earth. Complete with all the language, beliefs, and attitudes necessary to function in our society, our robot self usually gets us well into adulthood before we begin to awaken—if we ever do—to our higher awareness. Only then can we begin to understand that *we are caught in a mechanism that is not us*. But take heart! We can shed this spacesuit.

This robot self identifies mainly with the brain—"I think, therefore I am"—and is generally cut off from the instincts, emotions, and intuitions that would make it a more whole being. It controls the entire body/mind with an iron hand, reacting to its environment physically, mentally, and emotionally in a manner conditioned by its childhood experiences. While driving, for example, it may become infuriated when cut off by another driver, impatient at red lights, and anxious during traffic jams. In relationships, it is automatically attracted to people who remind it in some core way of its mother, father, or siblings and reacts to them as it did in childhood. It compulsively attempts to control the universe according to its own limited view of things, imagining that it alone knows what is right or wrong, bad or good. Imagining itself separated from the world at large yet responsible for running it, the poor robot mind often sows the seeds of its own destruction, becoming overstressed, isolated, and alone in its misery, much like our friend Ralph.

We who are dedicated to healing our rifts must become masters in our own homes by becoming *aware*. This special kind of awareness entails remembering our robot nature and developing a *witness self*, or *metacommunicator*, as it is called in psychology, that is dedicated to watching our false selves in action. For this it is very helpful to learn the art of meditation, which is called *centering prayer* in some Christian churches. The witness self is an unused part of our basic hardware that is capable of *being aware* of ourselves in action. We not only think and feel and act, but we can actually stand back and observe ourselves thinking, feeling, and acting. This process helps us discover who we are.

For example, as I write this page, I am aware of my breath catching as I search for just the right word. I am aware of my stomach wrenching slightly as my mind says, "You'd better write faster—not much time," and I feel a slight anxiety as my eyes glance at the clock. My fingers race. I notice my feet moving around under the table, participating in my anxiety by preparing for my escape. The fight-or-flight instinct is fully activated by my false self, which has automatically set itself into a panic mode by deciding—all on its own—that I should get so much writing done in such-and-such a time period. I observe it in wonder and admiration.

The false self, after all, is only doing the job it was trained to do by the folks in my early environment, who thought life was about success and failure, bad and good, winning and losing. If you are working, they taught, you should do as much as possible as quickly as possible or you will prove yourself lazy or a failure. It's the kind of outlook that led my father to kill himself when he could no longer compete. He had never been taught the spiritual point of view that life is about learning and growing—a playground for the soul.

I learned long ago that my robot self believes it must be anxious and fearful to do "a good job." So I watch it emerge as I do work of any kind. Are we ever free of the robot self's influences? Perhaps not. But through self-awareness we learn to choose the higher road and to enjoy our lives more fully. To achieve this I recommend this practice: Throughout the day and night, notice when you react physically, emotionally, or mentally to any stimulus, and notice also the assumptions of your conditioned mind. Though you may justify your reactions by saying, "They made me mad," or "Anyone would have felt that way," simply notice that tendency as well. Justifications are part of the trap. Your intention is but to find freedom by observing. Relax. It is a lifetime process. Soon you will do it as naturally as breathing. Awareness of the false self is an essential part of healing your rift. When the weeds are cleared from your garden, the fresh flowers of May can bloom.

Fertilizing the Flower of Self with Acceptance

Awareness must be nourished with *acceptance*. They go together like love and kisses. The ego self is tricky, you see. It learned its ways through the guilt, shame, and disapproval it received in childhood. It learned to judge and condemn whatever wasn't done "right." Therefore, as soon as your witness self becomes aware of a thought, attitude, or behavior, some part of you will jump in and condemn it: "Ah, look at that, will you! There you go again! You will never learn not to get angry in traffic. What an idiot you are!"

This will happen. It always does. And it is the great killer of awareness. After all, who would want to notice anything if they knew the reward would be immediate blame and punishment for doing so? That's how we learned to suppress our awareness in childhood, when we were too naive to recognize or do anything about it. We learned it at our parents' knees: "Don't do that! Bad girl! Naughty boy! Don't you ever learn? Don't do that again." We learned to treat ourselves in the same fashion—emotionally beating ourselves up for our mistakes— and we also learned to flinch from ourselves, hide our actions from our eyes, and pretend we didn't do it. It took some doing, but we finally succeeded in becoming *unaware*.

Predictably, our rugged friend Ralph had a very difficult time with acceptance. I heard him mumbling under his breath after our first session on awareness, and I asked him what he was thinking. At first he was unaware that he had been mumbling, but he gradually remembered: "I was telling myself that I probably won't be very good at this and I'd better concentrate. That's how I motivate myself. I tell myself I'll probably fail, then kick myself real hard when I do. It may not be right, Paul, but that's how I got where I am today."

It took a long time for Ralph to understand that his vicious treatment of himself was *exactly* how he got where he was—sick, tired, and on the verge of a breakdown! It was also the reason he was so unaware of himself. The only path to greater awareness is to accept whatever we see about ourselves. No, that does not mean we endorse our harmful actions or that we plan on doing them again. It simply acknowledges the truth that we cannot "beat it out of us." As Lincoln said, "A house divided against itself cannot stand."

I've yet to meet a client or student who took to acceptance and forgiveness of themselves naturally. Often the very exercise itself brings up a rage: "How dare I accept this horrible transgression? If I accept this thought or behavior, I will never be good enough, adequate, or lovable. I hate this aspect of myself. I'll never accept it. I'll continue to punish myself for it in every way possible." Can any of us thrive under such hatred and self-denial? We were taught by our early environment that such virulent self-punishment was the way to becoming better people. But guess what? It has never worked. And it reveals a huge wound that must be healed. Self-love and self-acceptance are important steps for healing our rift with God.

A friend and student, Bee, gave me a gift on a recent Sunday. She offered a spontaneous prayer of thanksgiving for learning awareness and acceptance: "Thank you, God, for that," she said. "For the first time in my fifty-nine years I am able to catch myself doing something destructive and not feel I have to beat myself up for it. Thank God I'm without shame and guilt! Now I can grow and become happier."

The Blessings That Awareness Brings Me

I have been teaching skills for inner awareness and acceptance for over twenty years. During those years, I have studied and practiced many tools for self-understanding, including Western psychology as well as the spiritual and psychological practices of Buddhism, Hinduism, Christianity, Judaism, Sufism, and shamanism. To be honest, I thought I knew something about self-inquiry and growth.

Then came an immense emotional and spiritual crisis that turned my life upside down. Fortunately, this time around, I was not as lost as I had been before my spiritual-awakening years in Utah. I had a deep sense of God, and I knew that I was taken care of in every way. But I was in pain. Some deep part of me felt lost, abandoned, unloved, and unredeemable. I knew that I was in for a long period of pain as I recovered from my loss, which seemed unbearable at times.

That's when my awareness and acceptance practice went to an entirely new level. With the pain as motivator, I relaxed my body deeply and asked that key spiritual question, over and again: "Who am I?" Gradually, more clearly than ever before, I became aware of the Truth that I am a son of God, that I, like everyone on the planet, was created in God's image and am filled with God's spirit. The Truth had always been there, and now my pain-motivated awareness was helping me to discover it more clearly than ever before.

That same awareness helped me see through my pain. As I sat in silence, I asked, "Who is it that is in pain?" My awareness cut like a knife to the real sufferer, and I discovered that the outer events of my life had simply uncovered an earlier wound which had never completely healed. When I asked who is in pain, I found a little boy who felt abandoned by his dead father. And with this new awareness I could at last bring love and acceptance to that old wound and take another important step in healing my rift with God.

As the Bible says, "Ye shall know the truth, and the truth shall make you free." Awareness is the handmaiden of truth, and its development is the stairstep to higher consciousness and our direct perception of God as our true nature.

EXPLORING OUR ASSUMPTIONS, BELIEFS, AND STORIES

When we have become dedicated to awareness, the fun can really begin. Remember, God is hidden within us, and awareness is the tool with which we look. We find that our True Nature, our Christ Consciousness, has been with us all along but has been obscured by the mind and our basic assumptions about ourselves and the world.

There's an ancient story that is told by many different spiritual traditions, always with a slightly different twist but the same meaning: Once upon a time there was a princess. She lost her way while walking deep in the woods one day and wandered into a foreign land. She walked for several days in search of home, falling down at times, tearing her clothing on underbrush, and becoming very tattered and disheveled. Finally, when she was on the brink of total collapse, she was found by some shepherds and brought to the new land. Weak and confused, she babbled on in her foreign tongue that she was a princess, but few could understand her, and no one believed that such a tattered and confused peasant could be a princess.

But some good people took pity on her, took her in, and taught the poor untalented girl to become a seamstress so that she might support herself. And after many months of hard work, she met a handsome village lad, fell in love, and married. She had long since given up her insistence that she was a princess, since people only made fun of her.

She gradually settled into village life. She had children, made a home for her family, and forgot about her life as royalty.

But her royal family, having never given up the search for their beloved daughter, continued to send courtiers far and wide in search of her. One day a trusted advisor to the king, one who knew and loved the princess, saw her at the village well and rushed to her, speaking in her native tongue. She barely recalled him or the language, so accustomed was she to her new life, but he was insistent and followed her home. There he pulled from his pouch a small painting of her in royal attire, reproduced for use in the royal search. He put it directly in front of her face and cried, "Behold, Princess, your true royal identity. Your father is ill and calls you home to claim your kingdom."

And with that, the princess realized that her humble role as villager, mother, and wife was but a small part of her real nature. Bringing her husband and children with her, she returned to the throne that was rightfully hers.

This story is about the deepest of all mysteries. We are and always have been children of God. Yet we gradually lose ourselves in the woods of life and forget our true identity. We forget our royal nature. In Aldous Huxley's *Perennial Philosophy*, which discusses the core spiritual teachings of all religions, he spoke of our struggle with our dual nature—human and divine—and asserted that the key ingredient of most spiritual systems is an attempt to transcend this duality and realize our divinity.

This process, however, requires us to see through the assumptions, stories, and beliefs we've been taught, which tell us that we are not spiritual at all. And this process of seeing through these is quite a job, indeed. When we came into the world, we knew nothing about how it operated. We had no assumptions, beliefs, or stories. We couldn't walk, talk, understand, or even feed ourselves. The first few years of our lives were a crash course in what to believe, how to live, and how to act, long before we had the ability to make conscious choices about what to accept as our own and what to reject.

Our *assumptions* about ourselves and life can be easily seen in the way we live our lives. When we walk with calmness and joyful expectation into a gathering of people we don't know, we probably have an inner assumption that people are friendly and mean no harm to us. If we are frightened and angry, we may have an assumption that people are critical and mean. If we start a new job or relationship with no fear and trepidation, we likely assume that we will meet with success and happiness. If we approach it anxiously and fearfully, we assume that we will fail.

Assumptions reflect our most deep-seated *beliefs* about ourselves, other people, and our relationship to the world in which we live. Einstein once said that the most important decision we have to make is whether or not the universe is friendly. *When we have a rift with God, we believe that the universe is not friendly. We believe that it is hostile or at best indifferent.* When we believe that the universe is unfriendly to us, we make an *assumption* that we are inadequate to deal with it effectively and that every encounter with life is fraught with danger.

That's where our *stories* come into play. Our beliefs lead us to assume that every interaction in life will conform to that belief, and so our minds automatically create stories to justify our assumptions. When Carl, for example, invited me to join him and some other friends for dinner on Saturday, I felt my introvert's fear of crowds rise up, and I nearly said, "No, thanks." Instead, I became aware of the fear that was driving me at the moment and noticed the inner story that had been automatically set off by the fear: "There'll be a lot of noise and a lot of shallow chatter. I will be uncomfortable and bored. I think I should stay home and prepare for the class I have next week."

My story about the gathering was a justification for following my fear, based upon my belief that I am not socially adept and that other people are shallow and boring. I was painfully shy as a child, and I was very uncomfortable with idle chatter. Therefore, my mind assumed that this evening's dinner party would be like that and automatically made up a story to match. The problem with it all, of course, is that Carl and my friends are not shallow and boring, I am no longer socially inept, and I was very hungry for social interaction just then. I told Carl I would be happy to join him for dinner.

Challenging Assumptions and Beliefs and Changing One's Stories

Brenda is a tall, strong woman with a well-developed male aspect that has driven her to both excellence and excesses in life. Her first comment when we met in my office was, "You could use some help on your direction-giving. I'll make up an easy-to-follow map for you to send to first-time clients and bring it in next time." Seldom have the first ten minutes with a student told me so much about her character.

Brenda was an iron woman, to say the least. Reared by a strong, hard-working, and hard-drinking father who demanded excellence from his children, Brenda learned early how to stand strong and earn his respect. She became just like him, only more so. She believed as he had taught that life was difficult and that the only way to show one's worth or to be secure was to work hard, stopping only to drink and party with equal fervor. She assumed that every person of worth believed the same as she did, and her constant story was, "I've got a lot of things to accomplish today, and if I don't do them something bad will happen, someone will be disappointed in me, and I'll be a failure."

After our first visit, I knew she would be a challenge. She was just recovering from breast cancer and knew on some level that her life depended on some sort of major inner change. But for the life of her, she couldn't figure out what that could be. Brenda, you see, believed with conviction all the beliefs, assumptions, and stories her father had told her. And as I pondered her situation, I felt an old sense of hopelessness settle over me. Suddenly, I knew she reminded me of my own life on the farm, and I realized that my father had believed in the same story line that was killing Brenda. Helping Brenda see through her stories to a script she could live with became very important to me.

Brenda stopped by to visit recently, some five years since our first meeting. She was just returning from a few months in Jamaica and was on her way to South America. Tan and fit, she plopped down on my couch and began recounting her life over the last year. She was as relaxed and peaceful as anyone I have ever met.

"You know, Paul, I never knew it could be like this," she said, waving her right arm for emphasis. "I haven't worked for two years, and I don't care if I ever do again. I've earned enough money with all that work over thirty years that I deserve to take it easy." She stopped for a moment of contemplation and then pondered aloud, "It shocked me when you pointed out that not all *good* people worked like I did, that a person can be worthwhile without working. Then you helped me see how I had come to believe that the meaning of life was work and drinking—that I had simply bought my dad's story. That was a revelation! Heck, I thought I was an independent thinker, but I was completely brainwashed into a belief that almost killed me. Thank God I'm free!"

Brenda's freedom means a lot to me. There's nothing wrong with work, of course, but when we make an idol of anything and hold it to be our reason for living, we enslave our soul and create a deadly rift with God. Inquiry was Brenda's chief means of discarding the false self and becoming free. And as she found freedom, I felt just a little bit of the sadness from my father's desperate act fall away from my heart.

Finding a Spiritual Vision

Brenda's courageous quest of self-inquiry led to a new story line in her life, a new myth to live by—an authentic *vision*. But she could never have accomplished this feat without a growing sense of who she really is, a sense of her spiritual identity. Very early in our work together, Brenda began to understand that her true identity is not her role in society—not mother, manager, hard worker, Californian, American— but the inner spirit, that which is within us all.

Finding out who we really are must *precede* our finding a vision to live by. Personal experience of God is necessary in healing the rift, because until we have had this experience—until we have felt it in our hearts—God is simply a memorized dogma of what we believe and has no personal connection with us. The scriptures tell us that without vision the people will perish. Our vision is our context for God, the vessel in which we carry and support our God-experience. But without the inner sense of who we are and how we relate to God, how are we to choose a vision that matches our innate nature? That would be like sending someone who had never heard music to judge a band competition.

Who were we, after all, before we could talk, before we assumed a role? And who will we be when we grow old and frail and work no more? All the cells in our bodies are replaced every year or so. Who are we if we aren't even our bodies? What is this energy, consciousness, and awareness that lives this short life upon the planet and then vanishes from view? These are the questions that Brenda put to herself over her years of awakening. And when she began to have a genuine sense of that Inner Christ and was able to follow it, she began her journey to find a vision for her spiritual life that would sustain her.

Learning to "Read God's Lips"

We often get caught up in our intellects and semantics and miss that in order to follow God's will in us what we need is *an experience of God.* Call our inner connection by any words that suit you—soul, atman, Buddha, Inner Christ, spirit. Just know that you are divine in nature and can have a direct daily experience of God that will heal and change your life. We have been told that God knows and cares about every hair on our bodies. Certainly, as we in the holistic health field can testify, this knowing and caring extends to our feelings, emotions, and thoughts; our body tensions and sensations; our dreams and visions, our energetic system—literally everything about us. Like snowflakes, we are each unique in our physical manifestation, and yet we are all of the same substance. And as we allow ourselves to know and express our uniqueness, we simultaneously come to know and express the One Spirit that inspires all of life.

As we learn how to "read God's lips," we will find many inner practices to assist us. The key ingredient in all of them is *inner focus,* because God is spirit, and the spirit of God is within all of us *as* us. Since God speaks through us and as us, we learn to know God by knowing ourselves. Therefore, the guidelines to spiritual recovery listed above will prove very helpful in this Self-knowledge. Inner awareness and acceptance are very important for the constant vigilance needed to escape the mind's addiction to the outer world of thoughts and things. And an awareness of our assumptions, beliefs, and stories will also help us with the mind's addiction and will help us stay adequately awake and in the moment to read God's lips.

The following are but a few of many practices that can help you keep an inner focus and learn to hear that *still small voice within*, whether it speaks through sounds, visions, dreams, bodily feelings, or coincidences. You may feel attracted to one or two of these practices, or you may find one not listed here that suits you better.

Meditation and Prayer

Tradition has it that prayer is talking to God and that meditation is listening to what She has to say back to you. I have found that the most effective method of prayer is one of sincerely and authentically talking to God as if to a best friend and of praying with an attitude of being *in God* rather than outside and remote. This helps us to develop an intimate inner relationship, one that keeps us aware of a constant inner presence guiding and keeping us. Prayers of gratitude are much more fulfilling than requests, for they acknowledge what we already have received and open the gates for more. We may call God's attention to an issue we believe to be important, but research shows that the most powerful prayer of all is "Thy will be done." Let God decide what is best in all circumstances.

Claire is a prayer superstar. Life is a constant prayer for her. Years ago, she read Brother Lawrence's *The Practice of the Presence of God* and has been doing so ever since. Every decision she makes is a prayer: "Lord, I'm thinking of going to the grocery. Is that the right thing to do?" She looks inside for a feeling of rightness or wrongness, and she follows it. She is always attuned to her body, mind, and emotions, so her prayers are always answered. They are an ongoing dialogue within her.

Claire has taught me a great deal about prayer. As I write this book, I constantly check within myself. Recently, at the suggestion of a friend, I ask, "Who is writing right now?" Sometimes it's God writing through me, which is the only way I want it to be. And sometimes I find that my mind has taken over and my writing has become an attempt to please others. I then silently ask God to take over again, asking that "Thy will be done."

Meditation is the handmaiden of prayer. Sometimes called *centering prayer* by some Christian groups, meditation is simply a method for going within, relaxing, and quieting the restless mind. Mystics of all traditions have noticed the subtle miracle that when we withdraw from the outer world of thoughts, forms, and activities, we encounter the Self, soul, spirit. God is truly within us all the time, and when we take the time each day for a period of silent contemplation, we obey the scriptural precept to "Be still, and know that I am God."

Meditation is also an ideal way to find the inner awareness we mentioned earlier. With a regular period of contemplation, we establish a felt sense of inner connection that lasts throughout the day. We are more calm and centered, more inwardly aware of how we wish to respond to the outer world. We know what we are feeling and thinking, and we know what old assumptions and stories our minds are projecting onto our present reality. We can ask, as I do with my writing, "Who is this that is doing my life right now?" If the answer is that an old story of inadequacy is on stage, you give her the hook and bring on the real star of the show—your True Self.

Dreams, Visions, and Divine Coincidences

Samuel is my personal hero in this aspect of Self- and God-awareness. Once he began to understand that he is far more than his thoughts and personal history, Samuel, a physicist by trade, applied his brilliant mind to reading God's lips.

"It's really quite simple, Paul," he explained to me. "I've spent my career studying invisible particles whose seemingly random movements can only be predicted by probability formulas. Well, of course, we humans are composed of the same stuff as the particles I've been observing for decades. The whole universe is. So why should I treat everyday life according to the old Newtonian model while knowing full well that the essence of life doesn't conform to it? In fact," Samuel continued, "I'll never get promoted for saying this publicly, but watching my dreams and inner images and cross-checking them with each other is a lot closer to the science I like to practice than that theoretical stuff in the laboratory."

Dreams come from the mystical, acausal unconscious, presenting images and dramas that reflect the inner meaning of our daily lives. With practice, we can establish an ongoing dialogue with our dreams and other unconscious material that will take us to a very deep and profound understanding of ourselves and God. Samuel found, as I do, that dreams are only one demonstration of the interconnectedness of all being and the deep mystery that everything is affected by each of us and that we affect everything else. Samuel's experience as a physicist led him to say, "But of course even we physicists know that!" when I explained that this is also the view of the mystics of all ages.

Samuel and I treat images, words, gut feelings, intuitions, and *divine coincidences* (Jung called this *synchronicity*) as the same phenomena as dreams—an aspect of reading God's lips. We duly note whatever occurs in the outer or inner world and cross-reference it with everything else, looking for probability patterns that reveal the inner nature of our existence, give us guidance in comporting our affairs, and show us the meaning of our lives.

Samuel, of course, has made a regular science out of this. He remembers his dream images, quite often sees them again during the events of the next day, and duly encounters a problem at work or in life for which that image is an answer. For example, he remembered a dream image of a man on the end of a plank that was extending from a building. On his way to work he noticed a seagull doing that very thing on a board at the end of a highway sign. And later at work, while stuck on a complicated problem, he remembered this image and realized he would have to "go out on a limb" to solve that problem. He immediately took a leap of faith in his thinking that gave him a very unpredictable but accurate answer. For Samuel, this was not an unusual happening.

Communing with Nature

Jill, a medical doctor, finds that windsurfing and hiking take her closer to her natural being than anything else.

"My work is so mental and stressful that I can't yet read God's lips anywhere else," Jill told me one day. "But when I'm out windsurfing, with the breeze in my face and the wind literally in my arms, I am entirely relaxed and completely attuned with myself and God. An hour of windsurfing brings me closer to God than a week of prayer and meditation. The same is true for hiking. Nature is obviously my spiritual practice."

Noticing the Body, Emotions, and Energy

Elementary-school teachers have found that people have very different modes of learning and so have learned to teach their students in the ways that they can actually learn. Shocking development, to let kids learn in the way that is natural for them, isn't it? I remember with pain those long days strapped to the chair performing endless hours of memorization and purely intellectual learning. What a chore it was for the emotional, energetic boy that I was! I learn best experientially, with my body and emotions firmly engaged. Let each learn as he or she can.

The same principle applies to reading God's lips to get to know yourself and God. Many of us are more emotional, physically kinetic, and aware of energy than others. For us, methods of body movement and of emotional and energetic awareness are helpful. As an emotional person, for example, I always felt judged by societal and spiritual groups, where emotions are not well received or tolerated. As I continued to work with myself and others, I realized that, whether we like it or not, emotions have to be accepted and dealt with. A passionate and emotional relationship with God is perfectly valid, after all, and essential for folks like me who experience a lot of emotions. It does no good to pretend they aren't there.

Jerry, my tai chi chuan instructor, taught me that the same is true for people who relate more to body movement and energetics. Until he began studying hatha yoga and tai chi, he had no way of relating to Self and spirit in his strongest suit: sensate movement and body energetics. As we worked, we found that what emotions were to me, body movement and energy were to him. They are our home, so to speak, and the way we can most effectively do our spiritual work. After a strong earthquake in our area, we compared notes: his way of recovering from the trauma of the quake was through tracking his body-energy shifts, while mine was awareness of my emotions. To each his or her own!

One could say that Jill, also, has chosen a physical route to reading God's lips. And Ralph, a first-year student of mine, finds that running in the morning does the same thing for him. Today, we are fortunate to have a plethora of means to engage the energetic and physical self for greater awareness. Hatha yoga, tai chi, and qi gong classes abound. And sports that allow us to be alone and introspective—while letting our bodies and energy systems relate to Self and God—are abundant as well. Like grade schoolers, we are best supported when we are learning in our natural way.

Finding a Mystical Vision

For most people I have accompanied through spiritual recovery—including myself—spiritual practice and evolution don't hold together without a clear mystical vision. I had lots of spiritual experiences during my time in Utah and after, but I had no clear vision, no physical teacher to guide me over the trail she knew because she had already traveled it, and no system to follow until I discovered one on my own. I had raw experience without a cohesive, comprehensive philosophy in which to hold it. I wouldn't trade that rough-and-tumble time of spiritual adventure for anything, but I see now that it was a lot more difficult and painful for me than necessary because I had no vision/receptacle for it.

The test for a spiritual vision is whether or not it feels right to our own Inner Self. That's it. Like the differences in modes of learning, we also have different ways of relating to vision. I recommend we honor that. When I went in search of a supportive vision, I visited every church, temple, or synagogue and investigated every spiritual vision I could find. I had no intention of joining a group which demanded that I or any other believe exactly as they did. I was on an inner journey to discover what felt right for me, but I actually didn't expect to find a group that fit for me. I was doing informational interviews, you might say—searching for the holy grail to hold my sacred wine.

But something strange happened for me that I have seen repeated with many of my students over the years. I found the centerpiece around which all the holy meals were arranged. In other words, I found that at essence all the teachings were saying the same thing. Only the outside looks different. Some of the priests and congregations had no spirit; others did. *But the deep mystical teachings all say the same thing, all bow to the same spirit. And if you get a roomful of true mystics from all those traditions together, they get along perfectly.*

In finding your vision, then, go to the center of your Self, get God from the inside, and then you can fit in anywhere, with any of the external visions of the same inner truth. It is definitely helpful to have a true vision for a container, and perhaps even a qualified teacher to give you guidance. Only make sure that you have done the work of seeing what fits with you and what does not. Honor this above all. And don't accept anything that has not been through the grinder of your own inner process. When you do, you may be ready to have not only a vision but perhaps a spiritual family as well.

CONNECTING IN RELATIONSHIP AND COMMUNITY

"Look, Paul," Myrtle said, looking very determined and angry. "I just don't do groups. OK? It's a big step for me to let anyone into my life to help. You're my teacher and counselor. We're doing very well together, and that's a big deal for me. So don't push it."

Myrtle's a strong and determined woman. It took a lot for me to push this point a bit further, but I felt I had no choice. She had made good progress in many areas of her life and had developed a strong and loving relationship with God. But she had huge, unresolved social

issues and remained isolated. She was deeply afraid of people, especially groups, and vigorously avoided them. Yet she was painfully
lonely and unhappy in her isolation. I wanted her to try to parlay her
new relationship with God into a more loving relationship with her fellow humans.

I also empathized deeply with Myrtle. Until fifteen years ago, when
I began my vision search, I also had avoided groups, though I don't
think I was nearly as afraid of them as was Myrtle. Now I recognize
how painfully isolated and lonely I really was. We humans have varying
degrees of need for social and community interaction, of course, but
studies show that good health comes from our interacting with spiritual communities, indicate our innate need for them. As with many
things, our fears and our minds' stories keep us from something we
need very much.

I have heard spiritual leaders like Mother Teresa talk of the great
social and spiritual poverty we have in the West, and now I too can
see it. After all, as Samuel, our scientist, sees so clearly, we are
all interconnected. "No man is an island, entire of itself," said John
Donne. "Every man is a piece of the continent, a part of the main."
Traditional societies were tribal in nature, and most cultures retain
traditional extended families in which everyone has a part and all
belong to the whole. These societies experienced themselves as
immersed in nature, and their religious life reflected a sense of
participation in a larger whole. Spirituality and connectedness
were one.

Something beautiful can happen for us when we find a truly loving
and accepting spiritual group within which to interact and flower. We
find ourselves reflected in other people, and we learn about ourselves
as we learn about them. We find that these *others* are just like us, afraid
of the same things and stuck with the same low self-esteem and the
same sense of inadequacy. As we learn to love and accept them, seeing
in them how unnecessary it is for *us* to feel inadequate and suffer for
it, we learn to love and accept ourselves. And through that mutual love
and acceptance we begin to feel the love of God flowing through it all.
We begin to feel at home in the universe.

You see, to the divine aspect of our inner nature, everything and everyone we encounter *is* God. Until we get to know others, we tend to project onto them all the ideas and prejudices that were taught to us—that, being part of a hostile universe, people are basically out to get us and are basically unfriendly, judgmental, and mean-spirited. We act as if our perceptions are true, and sure enough, we confirm our theory: God, other people, and the universe itself remain unfriendly to us.

But when we join a spiritual community and actively engage in it as a contributing and supporting member, we may actually begin to feel that we at last belong to a healthy and loving family. We feel that we belong to something bigger than ourselves. This group may also have a strong vision that matches our own, which adds to our sense of belonging and common cause. In time, we begin to feel safe and loved in the world.

This sense of being loved and protected in the spiritual community becomes the feeling you experience in your relationship with God. You begin to *feel* loved and protected and supported by God. And because God is also this interactive universe the physicists describe, we increasingly attract to us those very experiences, which of course increase the feelings of being loved and protected—and which attract more of the same. As mystics everywhere will tell you, "Whatsoever a man thinketh in his heart, so is he."

A young student at a recent retreat reported at the outset that she felt insecure and inadequate and certain that people wouldn't like her and would reject her. Sure enough, at a key point in the weekend, after sequentially acknowledging everyone else, I unintentionally failed to acknowledge her. It was one of those *divine coincidences* I mentioned earlier, an opportunity given by God for her benefit. When she later told me how rejected and hurt she had felt, I consoled her, but I also reminded her that she had expected at the beginning that she would feel this way.

She thought about it long and hard and later told me, "I think I understand now. All through the weekend people have been loving and accepting toward me, but I somehow never took it in. They must be pretending to like me, or perhaps I have them fooled in some way. But when you forgot to acknowledge me, I thought, 'Oh yes, there it is at last. I *knew* they didn't like me!'" She smiled softly, but there was a strength in her eyes. "Now I see what you've been saying, Paul. I feel loved and accepted today for the first time, and I'm going to keep that feeling, because the love in this group has proved to me that I'm lovable. I won't let my old story take over again."

FINDING SELF-RESPONSIBILITY
FOR HEALTH AND SPIRIT

I feel in my heart one particular desire for my readers: that they understand there is no real separation between spiritual health and physical, emotional, and mental health. We are made of the same stuff and substance as the rest of the universe. There is no separation anywhere. Our whole being suffers when we never exercise, and it also suffers when we have no spiritual life. When the waters of spirit are dammed up so that they no longer flow in our lives, our crops suffer accordingly. As above, so below. And we as individuals are ultimately the only ones who can be responsible for keeping these spiritual waters flowing in our lives. Self-responsibility for health and spirit is essential for healing your rift with God.

Bernice got very angry with me at a spiritual retreat she attended recently. A tall, cheerful woman by nature, she was appalled to find herself so angry for no apparent reason. She withdrew from the rest of us and took long walks, even skipping without warning one or two of our key sessions. I could see this was happening, knew it was important, and kept my distance. Bernice had always been a "good student" who would never miss a session without a good reason. I might have called a more lax person to task for this, but not Bernice. She was onto something good.

She came into my office for a private interview some days after the retreat, mortified at what she felt was her "inexcusable rudeness." Bernice was a perfectionist and couldn't bear not doing things *right*.

After all, she had criticized many people many times for doing what she had done. Yet for all that, she was still mad as hell.

"I don't know what's going on with me, Paul," she said, holding her head in her right hand while looking at the floor, her left fist clenched, "but I'm still pissed at you. I've been so good on the spiritual path for so long. I've done everything you recommend to a T and I've benefited a lot. But when you spoke at the retreat, I felt I'd had enough. It reminded me of school and work and how hard I always try to do what the teacher or boss or doctor tells me I should do. I'm just sick of trying to be good!"

"Congratulations!" I said, feeling like a new father. "I'm so glad you are sick of all that stuff. I couldn't be happier. Now we can finally begin the spiritual path."

"What are you talking about?" Bernice said, confused and shocked. She obviously expected that I would be angry with her for breaking the rules. Bernice has an innocence about her that is her saving grace. She touches me deeply with that innocence, helping me to contact my own. She was at a key place in her spiritual growth, one that needed special care. I prayed for guidance in choosing my words well, and I leaned forward to touch her clenched left hand.

"Being good and following the rules someone else hands to you is not being yourself, Bernice," I said. "I know you've built your life on *being good* and *doing it right*, so this may not be an easy concept to swallow. It's rather frightening. But I welcome your anger at me. I'm the last in a long line of people who *seem* to have expected you to be good and do it right. You're not so much mad at me as mad at feeling like you have to be something other than who you are to be accepted and loved. Whether you're late or early, whether you're angry, spiteful, cheerful, or sad, everyone in our group, including me, loves you as you are. And now it's time for you to rebel against us and find that out for yourself."

"Oh God," she said, tearfully. "I can't believe this. I can see it so clearly as you say it, but I still can't believe it. I have to find God on my own terms, don't I? I can't do it by trying to be perfect or by pleasing you. I have to find out who I am, and then I'll know who God is. God help me."

I'm pleased to say God *did* help Bernice. She took a break from our spiritual group and did a lot of searching on her own, checking in with me periodically to make sure she wasn't "doing it right," that she was doing it *her* way. Everyone noticed she was different after that—even the healthcare practitioners she occasionally visited. She was no longer looking for experts to tell her what was right. She was in touch with her own inner authority, and although she asked for health and spiritual clarification, she took her own advice from then on. Bernice finally found her own self-responsibility for health and spirit, and as Robert Frost said about taking the road less traveled, "that has made all the difference."

The Road to Self Is through the Inner Authority

Time and again in my work I find people like Bernice who have been conditioned to believe—despite being told a thousand times to look inward for the answer—that God, health, and wholeness lie outside themselves and can only be attained through some external authority. They fall in love over and over again with the hand that points them to themselves, failing to understand that the map is not the territory and the pointing finger is not God. These people attend classes to take notes and memorize the facts that some authority tells them, go to doctors to get fixed, and go to churches to follow the rules and beliefs handed to them. They have great difficulty understanding that they must become their own authority and follow their own path.

Faith is essential for embracing God, health, and wholeness. Hope is vital. Love is absolutely necessary. But nothing is more important than finding our own authority and following that above all. We are children of God, after all, and each of us has the wisdom of God within us that is perfectly suited to the individual state of our unique minds, bodies, and spirits. Like fingerprints and snowflakes, we are very much like our brothers and sisters, and we are also unique. When we learn to trust our Inner Wisdom, it will tell us what's right for us. If we do not, we are lost. It's as simple as that, for trusting our Inner Wisdom is the same as trusting our souls or trusting God. We learn to do so or we perish.

This does not mean that we eliminate the "experts" and spiritual teachers and groups. It means that we develop a different relationship with them. They no longer tell us what to do; they offer guidance and give recommendations. We listen sincerely, and if our health is at stake we obey orders until we can get a second and third opinion. If they all agree, we will probably follow their advice. If not, *we* will decide whose advice to follow. I recently heard a health speaker say that most breakthroughs come because someone rejected all the experts and sought some brand-new answers. But whatever we choose to do, we will always consult our Inner Wisdom, for we know that passive dependency on outer authority endangers the body *and* soul.

All five of our basic guidelines to spiritual recovery find their foundation in self-responsibility, for all are predicated upon an individual search for Truth, for Self, and God. We may use resources to find Self and God, but at a certain point we must learn to trust our Inner Wisdom. Only then can we fully heal our rift with God.

~ 6 ~

COMMON OBSTACLES
TO HEALING THE RIFT

DURING THE SEARCH for my own path to spiritual recovery, I have found many helpful tools and skills that I have shared in the preceding pages. Just as these helpful guidelines are important to our growth, however, there are also behaviors and thought processes that inhibit the soul growth we are seeking. These inhibitors are often mirror images of the helpful guidelines, and remember that mirrors often help us see things about ourselves that we can't see and/or don't want to see.

I have heard many ministers and spiritual teachers say that only a small percentage of the people who hear them actually *get* what they are teaching and apply it to their own spiritual vision. The rest are followers, either projecting perfection onto these teachers or wandering off in search of someone who does have the "true" teaching. Followers such as these do not understand that the true path is found not through blind belief but through inner discovery. They avoid the inner search by letting their teachers do it for them. And, of course, no one *can* do that for any of us, though a good teacher can chart the territory.

All too many sincere seekers fail in their search for no other reason than the fact that the only path they know won't take them where they want to go. Many teachers and ministers are aware of this problem and search for ways to help people to become true students, ones who understand that spiritual growth and healing are not about who they follow but about what they *become* through the teachings. Again, the best way of teaching this is often by pointing out the opposite—"Not this, not that." No matter how intensely one longs for God, he or she must be aware of the obstacles on the spiritual path in order to heal the rift with God.

Riding the Big Horse

At a recent spiritual retreat, as we were discussing the obstacles on the path, a student offered this wonderful analogy of a style of horse-back riding called *dressage* he had just started: "This new style," he said, "makes you unlearn old habits. I've got a new horse that knows the new style quite well. He's big, powerful, and very responsive to the rider. The problem is that *I* don't know the style very well and am always making mistakes. Because the horse does know it, we don't get along.

"The style reminds me a lot of what you're describing about the spiritual path, Paul. Basically, you have to learn how to be very inwardly focused, very self-aware: to be calm inside, to know what your emotions are and keep them calm; to be aware of your body tension and relax; to keep totally balanced on the horse; to keep your mind clear and in the present moment instead of thinking about something else; and to be totally loose and surrendered to what the horse is doing without interfering in any way. The main learning for me is how to do all that calm, inward stuff while all the while knowing that this big horse can catapult me like from a slingshot any moment.

"So most of it," he said, shaking his head in awe, "is avoiding the obstacles, just like in spiritual growth, but you're motivated a lot by the instant feedback you get from the horse. If I'm afraid, he'll pick it right up and take over. If I'm all tense or unbalanced, he'll shift around to compensate and mess up the whole routine. And if I'm not totally in the moment, present with what is happening, he'll pick that up too and we're off-kilter.

"The point is," he said, pausing for emphasis, "whatever attitude, emotion, thought, tension, or imbalance in the rider is immediately fed back to him by the horse. Since he is so well-trained, it *seems* as though he's in charge because he does the routine while the rider just surrenders and doesn't interfere. But actually, the rider is in charge by his excellence of surrender. Do you see what I mean?"

"Tell us more about how this applies to the spiritual path," I requested, excited by the analogy.

"That horse is no different from the rest of nature, from life, or from God," he replied excitedly. "God, as our Inner Spirit, knows how to handle our lives and is doing it all the time, whether we know it or not. Everything is in Divine Order, and if we recognize it and surrender, just sending in minor surrendered requests from time to time, God will continue the routine of abundance and grace for all. The routine only breaks down because of our self-made obstacles, not God's. When things fall apart it's not because God forgot the routine; it's because we're out of balance.

"So, everything we think, feel, the way we carry ourselves in life, our expectations and assumptions—they're all the messages we're sending out to God, just like with the horse. If we're upset at somebody, feeling like a victim and hating them, God responds to that and we get more of it. If we're tense and off-balance, God responds to that, too. If we feel inadequate and not good enough, the same.

"But if we are very aware and accepting of ourselves as we talked about this morning, if we know we're loved and loving, if we take responsibility for ourselves and are calm and relaxed, the horse—I mean God—will respond to that also, and we'll get more of it. The trick is to stay cool, calm, balanced, and surrendered." John shrugged his shoulders and smiled. "It's so clear to me. I wish all of you could go riding with me and see for yourself."

"We are, John, we are," someone else said, and we all laughed, knowing that the analogy holds together quite well. Most of the group members live and work in a crowded high-tech area of fast-paced living. We all ride the big horse every day, and we know the difficulty of staying calm and surrendered in the midst of it all. The fast pace of the area increases our tendency to get lost in it all and lose our surrendered nature. We need to be aware of the obstacles as much as John does.

THE FIVE COMMON OBSTACLES TO HEALING THE RIFT

The obstacles to healing the rift are the same as the obstacles to success on any spiritual path, because in their essence all paths ultimately lead to total union with God, our True Self. The factor that underlies all of these obstacles is our mind. Ironically, the very tool that has made us successful in dealing with the world makes us totally incompetent when it comes to connecting with God. As the old farmer says to the tourist asking for directions to the next town: "You can't get there from here." In our case, we can't get our rift healed by using the systems, structures, and judgments that created the rift in the first place.

A Sufi story of a drunken drummer, a devout but misguided student, and a great teacher exemplifies this fact. The devout student followed his master for decades, serving him, defending him, and announcing his greatness to the world wherever they traveled. He had every right to hope that when the master ascended to God, he, the faithful student, would be taken along. Finally, when that day seemed near, the pair stopped at an inn for food and were harassed mercilessly by a drunken drummer, who made no end of noise and rude comments. The student's attempts to protect the master were in vain, and when the pair left for a walk on some nearby sea cliffs, the drummer followed, beating his drum and singing.

Finally, on the edge of the cliffs, the master stopped, and spreading his magic carpet out before them, he prepared to ascend to God. As he stepped onto the carpet, he smilingly invited the drummer aboard, and the carpet lifted the pair above the earth, leaving the devout student behind.

"Master, wait, what is this?" cried the student in despair. "Now that it is time to see God, you leave me behind and take this drunken drummer? Have my years of service meant nothing to you? Why not take *me* to God?"

"Because this man was meant to go with me," said the master, dispassionately, "while you are unteachable."

With a slight flick of his head, the master pulled the drunken drummer to his bosom and the carpet lifted high above the cliffs and disappeared. The downcast student spent his remaining days trying to understand his master's last teaching. It is said, however, that at the moment of death he looked up toward heaven, his smiling face illumined by some invisible light, and said, "Ah, yes. Now, master, I understand."

Perhaps, as we read the five obstacles to healing our rift, we will all begin to more fully understand what obstacles render us unteachable and thus unable to gaze flush into the face of God.

The five obstacles are *being the perfect student, taking a spiritual bypass, cutting a deal with God, fear of the new and powerful,* and *gaining the world and losing the self.* All of these obstacles are creations of the conditioned mind seeking to maintain the status quo. After all, when we finally rise on our own "magic carpets" and gaze into the face of God, we will understand at last with St. Paul and the devout student that "now we see through a glass, darkly."

BEING THE PERFECT STUDENT

No one is more angry and discontent with spiritual teaching than the perfect student. Having succeeded at school and in the material world through intellectual understanding, memorizing dogmas and rituals, arguing points and following rules, this student expects the same results on the spiritual path. When that expectation is, hopefully, not fulfilled by the teacher, the perfect student becomes mad as hell and may even leave that church or teacher in search of a group where his or her strategies will elicit the approval and credit she seeks. She has no idea that these strategies are merely her "ego's plan for redemption," as *A Course in Miracles* puts it, that they are counterproductive for reaching the kingdom of God. It is part of a teacher's job to make sure these egocentric strategies fail so that the student goes beyond them. Most students I've encountered understand this truth sooner or later.

But Howard never did. When he arrived in the spiritual group I belonged to, he behaved like a *wunderkind*—sincere, devoted, and very interested in all the facts and details that he could wrap his mind around. Though clearly a beginner, he was a joy to his teacher. But Howard could not grasp that spiritual growth is not about memorization and information but about transformation, about apprehending what our egos perceive as an upside-down reality from the one our minds know, a reality where, according to the Bible, "the last shall be first and the first shall be last."

"When are we going to have more information and ritual?" Howard asked our teacher one night. "You keep asking us to discuss how we're dealing with our lives, and I don't like that. I want some new material or I get bored. I want to be challenged!"

"Well, you see, Howard, that's your fixation—facts, information— and it serves you well in the high-tech industry where you work," she explained. "But here you seek *higher awareness*, which by its very definition means beyond your egocentric fixation. We ask you to apply these spiritual tools to your life and notice what happens. This kind of learning is not meant to reinforce your ego but to help you see life from a spiritual perspective."

Howard, bless him, did not understand this any more than the devout student in the Sufi story above. He was unteachable. He got angry, and ultimately—not getting his way—he went off in search of a teacher who would fulfill his expectations. And this is fine and as it should be. I feel confident that Howard will learn this very hard lesson one day, the lesson that being a perfect student will not get him to God. But he will have quite a few lessons along the way before he gets it.

Mystics of all traditions agree that there are two kinds of knowledge and two kinds of students to go with them. The first and lower kind of knowledge is of an academic sort, science and philosophy and even knowledge of the scriptures. The students of this knowledge were the "scribes" discussed in the New Testament, who quoted scriptures but had no personal experience of God. The second and higher form of knowledge is immediate personal experience of God. As we recall, the

scribes and others were amazed that Jesus spoke "as one having authority" rather than quoting from texts. Students who find this higher
knowledge—and Christ told us that we *will* find if we so seek—
become teachers who do not need ponderous volumes of information
because they teach from inner experience of Truth.

Transforming the "Perfect Student" into the "True Student"

The *perfect student* in us must be transformed into the *true student*. We
got our concept of the perfect student from our parents, schools,
and society, who taught that learning was an intellectual process
resulting in high marks and a gold star for good performance. What
we *became* through our learning was secondary to our being able to
prove to our teachers that we were understanding and remembering
their lessons.

When I was a college writing instructor, all that my students
wanted to know was how they would be graded. Learning didn't
matter to them. They became confused and angry when I told them
they would be graded on how well they learned to think for themselves and write about what they thought. They had been taught to
regurgitate facts, not to think for themselves. When spiritual students try to pull that same, time-honored trick of performing for
approval, they doom themselves to a lifetime of being scribes, and
they will watch from the cliffs as the drunken drummer sails off with
the master to God.

To be successful in our search for God, we must transform this cul-
turally conditioned perfect student into the true student. All true
teachers recognize true students and revere them, for true students
and true teachers are two sides of the same coin. A true teacher is none
other than a true student who has begun to teach others how to learn
the higher knowledge of spirit.

Every true student knows that life and all experience is her teacher.
When Josette found herself angry one morning at a neighborhood
gardener for his loud leaf blower, she learned a great deal about her
controlling mind and how it wants things perfectly quiet. She also

learned that she could be aware of her anger and that by taking a deep breath and acknowledging it, she could relax and accept noise as a part of life. By embracing her anger, she entered a state of peace, love, and acceptance, which is the fruit of the spirit. She was being a true student by learning to transform herself through the teaching of life, her teacher.

The true student may read scriptures, but through a different lens than the perfect student. The true student reading Christ's Sermon on the Mount will understand something very different from the perfect student when they both read, "For I say unto you, That except your righteousness shall exceed the righteousness of the scribes and Pharisees, ye shall in no case enter into the kingdom of heaven." The true student will know that Christ speaks of the narrow-mindedness and intolerance of those who cling to external forms and dogmatic, intellectual interpretations of scriptures, and he will look within himself for these obstacles to spiritual growth. A perfect student, motivated by "getting it right," will understand no such thing. For her, the statement will make no sense.

"You can't get there from here," said the farmer to the tourist, and isn't this the message of the above Beatitude? The ego's strategies are of no use on the spiritual path. God is beyond all our concepts of right and wrong, good and evil. Since each of us is a manifestation of the One Spirit, we must each find God within ourselves through inner experience. The attitude of the perfect student is the worst of all obstacles to healing our rift with God because it takes us on the road to the ego's idea of heaven, which is sheer illusion. And if we take that route, we "shall in no case enter into the kingdom of heaven."

TAKING A SPIRITUAL BYPASS

We all love a bypass. We just don't like to deal with the details that seem to get in the way of where we're going. If I'm headed for the mountains, I will take a bypass around any city along the way. My computer engineers tell me they use a "work-around," a sort of bypass until a later date of problems they don't want to deal with in their computerized systems. We are goal-oriented, and we can't conceive that in many cases the step-by-step working through what we may perceive as obstacles may actually be the only way of getting there at all.

An old spiritual story makes this point very clear. An impatient academic approached a mystic, seeking immersion in the Divine. After a few moments, the academic asked the fateful question: " How long will it take, Master?"

"Expect ten years," the master calmly replied, "if you practice diligently."

"Oh, but Sir," said the appalled seeker, "we academics know how to apply ourselves to learning. I myself am a doctor of philosophy who already knows all the scriptures quite well. Surely I can bypass some of the basics. How long will it take me?"

"Oh, yes, quite so," said the master with sincerity. "You make a very good point. For you, fifteen years."

This master obviously understood how great an obstacle is the spiritual bypass. Such a person, like the perfect student, makes the false assumptions that he knows what a spiritual path is all about and that the details everyone else has to follow do not apply to him. He wastes most of his vital time and effort looking for a way to get around the work required to "get there from here," not understanding that the *process* is the learning.

In many cases, that process is getting to know our personality before we try to transcend it: "Know thyself." Most of us would subscribe to this truth, but we apply it more easily to other people than to ourselves. We, after all, know ourselves, don't we? I don't believe we do, actually. In fact, in my experience, the wisest among us are the first to admit that they know very little about themselves and are extremely dedicated to finding out more. They know that unless we watch our foibles very closely, we will get bitten by them. And we—whether Christian, Jew, Hindu, Buddhist, or Muslim—have watched many well-known teachers be pulled into the muck by personality defects that they evidently thought they could bypass.

Most people who seek the spiritual bypass are in considerable pain because of mental and emotional issues but don't want to deal with them. Drawn to the spiritual path, which often appears to be the very bypass they've been seeking, they hear and read about spiritual ecstasy and want *some of that*. Many of these folks are even able to achieve high spiritual states by bypassing their minds and emotions. These are the unlucky ones. The higher they climb the spiritual ladder and receive recognition for it, the harder it is for them to look for the snake in their boot, a poisonous snake that will undo them and the paradise they have built.

Esther was one such person. A highly spiritual person from her childhood, she was a rebel against religion who turned to alcohol in her teens. She had come to me originally to deal with deep resentments against her parents and her husband before admitting that she had an alcohol problem. After working with me for a short while, she quit drinking, joined AA, and stopped seeing me. Ten years later, when she called for an appointment, she was a well-known speaker and writer in the AA field and was considered a role model for thousands of people in recovery.

"But I feel like such a phony, Paul," she said, after telling me a bit about her journey since we had last met. "I started working on my anger and resentments with you, but after I found God and started AA, I just didn't think it was necessary. I was sure the program and God were enough. After all, I turned my life over to God.

"I really worked the AA program very hard. I became a sponsor for others right away because people could see that I *got it*, but it wasn't long before I could see that I still had that anger and resentment problem. I'm a pretty miserable person, to tell the truth about it.

"I think that's the real problem for me, what gets me stuck," she said, studying the carpet before her intently. "I've become a big role model for the program and for faith in God. People turn to me for advice and support. I feel I'd be letting them down if I confessed to being a miserable SOB. I'm afraid to talk about my own pain, so it just gets worse. I'm here to get help before I start drinking again."

Esther was in tears by then, and I wasn't far from it. Her story touched me deeply, because I've been there, too, along with thousands of other caregivers, ministers, and teachers. I remembered the painful years after my spiritual awakening when I, too, realized that my sudden awakening had bypassed much-needed emotional work. Like Esther, I had felt that spiritual awakening was all I *should* need in order to handle everything in life. I was sorely mistaken.

Some teachers point out that we need to approach spiritual healing on two levels: that of technology and that of content. Spiritual technology consists of the methods that each spiritual tradition teaches for realizing God, such as prayer, meditation, spiritual reading, and the like. Content is the "stuff" of our personalities—the issues like Esther's anger or my own feelings of abandonment—that consistently raise their ugly heads and beg to be reckoned with.

We cannot bypass our issues with immunity. Nor need we become so engrossed in them that we lose sight of our spiritual goals. When Esther began to acknowledge her bypassed emotions and began working with them with awareness and acceptance, she soon found that she was stronger on her spiritual path than ever and could be a truly healthy model for those at Alcoholics Anonymous who sought her help.

CUTTING A DEAL WITH GOD

Bill was absolutely furious. He sat with his arms folded, glaring at the floor. Since this was not something I normally encounter in my class on soul awareness, I was somewhat taken aback. I thought at first he was angry with me, but he said later he was furious with God "for not keeping his side of the bargain."

"I started this class with high intentions," he said bitterly. "I could see that I wasn't living right, and I figured if I straightened out, so would my life. Well, it hasn't worked out that way. I'm still losing the business I was trying to save by turning to Him, and my wife's still gone. I feel I've been betrayed by God, and I'm mad as hell! This might be my last night here with you people. This stuff just doesn't work."

After praying, meditating, exercising, and eating right for six weeks, Bill could see no change in his business or his love life. His wife of ten years had left three months before. His sales were almost nonexistent. He was feeling depressed and had been drinking heavily. He could understand things not going right when he was "messing up." But he'd made a *deal with God* and had been doing all the right things. Now, why weren't things going right?

"You're acting like a petulant child, Bill," Alice told him. "You remind me of my five-year-old who acts like a good little boy three weeks before Christmas to make sure he gets lots of presents and then throws a tantrum if he doesn't get everything he asked for." Alice was a bit angry. A plainspoken woman with three children, she did not spare Bill the rod in the least.

"God doesn't cut deals any more than I do with my kids. You can't manipulate God into giving you what you want, Bill. You made the agreement up; He didn't agree to it. God wants your heart, your love, your surrender. He wants you to transform yourself, to open your heart and sincerely search out your faults and correct them. You won't get anywhere till you get sincere about it and quit trying to cut deals with God."

Alice is tougher than I am on people, but she was right on about Bill. When people who are carrying a lot of baggage in their backseat suddenly hit the brakes, everything tends to rush forward and hit them in the backside. That's what had happened to Bill. He had held back all of his baggage with alcohol and irresponsible behavior, and when he stopped all of that for an interlude of right living, the baggage came hurtling forward. He began to feel his neediness and resentments and express them at God. With our help, Bill began to see that it was a good thing to get his surfacing baggage out in the open where he could see and deal with it. He began to work sincerely on himself and quit trying to manipulate God.

"Alice was right about me," he said. "I had an immature attitude about life and about God. I was still operating out of that Sunday-school mentality of the Big Daddy in the Sky with the computer, jotting down 'good boy' or 'bad boy.' I put the responsibility for my life *out there* rather than *in here*. God does not cut deals. I see that, now."

Bill's case may seem extreme, but I meet people every day who are disillusioned because their chosen course of action doesn't seem to be working. Dieters are the best examples. We follow the latest and greatest eating plan, hoping to lose those ten pounds in ten days like the magazine article said, and when it doesn't happen that way, we get mad as hell. So what do we do? Exercise a little more or eat less? No, we feel betrayed and use the excuse to eat everything in sight. We feel somehow justified in our self-destructive eating because we feel we were somehow cursed by God with an inefficient metabolism.

But the people who have turned to God to put their lives back in order tend to be the most attached to cutting a deal.

"He hates me, Paul. That's all I can figure," said Rex, shoving his long hair back with both hands. "I'm broke, I can't hold a job, and I can't find a woman who'll have me. Everyone said to turn my life over to God, and I did. But he's dropping the ball. Damn it, Paul, I'm hurting here. What the hell am I doing wrong?"

I listened to Rex with compassion. He was following his usual pattern, and I asked his higher wisdom to help him see his erroneous thinking. Whenever things went well for Rex—whenever he got what he wanted—he praised God enthusiastically. But when things went wrong, God was a bum. At the point of our conversation, God had been a bum for six weeks. Rex would begin each week's session by complaining about God's perfidy. And each week I would do my job by helping him to see a wider picture of God's grace. He would leave after our hour feeling much better. But when the next week came he was in the same complaining mood. What would it take, I wondered, to break this cycle of cutting a deal with God? A novel idea came to me: Tell him the truth.

"I'm feeling a little defeated here, Rex. I'm not sure anymore that I'm the person to help you with this," I said, feeling quite sad. "Each week you come in here and complain that God has broken your contract. Each week I tell you that the God I know doesn't sign contracts. You say you've surrendered your life to God, but you obviously have not or you wouldn't be second-guessing Her all the time. But I've told you all this before. You seem to agree but then go right back into it. Evidently whatever I'm doing isn't working."

Rex looked perplexed, a little frightened. He and I had become very close, and I knew he depended on me to keep his emotions in balance.

But was our relationship still valid? Was I really helping him if he kept returning to his old pattern? It was time to find out. I got up, paced around, and then returned to my chair. I waited for him to respond.

"I feel like I've disappointed you, Paul. But I'm just trying to understand. I don't mean to let you down."

"I understand, Rex. This isn't about me and whether I feel let down. This is about you and what's good for you," I said. "I want to help you, and if I'm not helping I want to get out of the way and let someone else do the job. You came to me to help you heal this resentment you have against God. That's *our* deal. And I tell you, week after week, that the biggest obstacle I can see to your healing this resentment is your concept of God, that God is supposed to act like some sort of trained dog and fetch the paper for you every morning. This is an immature view of God that you will have to recognize and consciously shift to a more adult level. Unless you're willing to take responsibility for doing this job, I can't help you."

The truth always works best, even if what happens isn't necessarily what we *want* to happen. In Rex's case, my truth had a greater effect than I could have anticipated. By mutual agreement, we took a five-week break, with the understanding that we would resume our sessions only if he was ready to break his old making-a-deal habit. He came back a changed man. Together we plunged into his resentments against God and found a small, angry, abused child whose anger toward his parents and his church had become resentment at God. He was actually a true believer of the rebels-against-religion type.

As we worked, Rex realized that his resentment toward God was symptomatic of an immaturity prevalent in all of his life, especially his work and love relationships. He had felt this same deep-seated resentment toward all of his bosses and romantic partners. He'd even felt this way toward close friends. He wanted others to be responsible for him. This immaturity had slipped into his relationship with me and was the reason he had stopped making progress. With this new understanding and self-responsibility, Rex went on to a new phase of his life, gradually developing an adult relationship with God as well as with the people at his work and in his outside friendships.

Becoming an Adult

The core issue underlying our tendency to make a deal with God is immaturity. Mature adults take responsibility for themselves and do not feel or believe that anyone else is obliged to do it for them. The immature of all ages either want or expect others to take care of them. More likely than not, the let's-make-a-deal folks did not get their needs met in a responsible manner as children, and they remain stuck in the childish "I'll be good if you'll get me a new toy" attitude mentioned above by Alice. Any of us reared in the grading-and-rewards system based on being "good boys and girls" is prone to this immature attitude to some degree. And we suffer because of it.

As Alice said, God does not make deals. When we try to make a deal with God, we assume the arrogance that we—our egos—know what is best for us, and we clearly do not. Even scientific research, long the opponent of faith, demonstrates clearly that the most powerful and effective prayer is "Thy will be done." *True* faith is in a higher power, a cosmic intelligence beyond our understanding. When we truly surrender to that power, we turn our lives and affairs over to God's keeping. We acknowledge our "preference" for desired outcomes, and then we surrender all outcomes to God, trusting in and accepting all outcomes.

Strangely, many people will see this trust and surrender as an even more immature and dependent attitude than the let's-make-a-deal approach. They see surrender as a shirking of responsibility. Not so. This surrender is based on the highest possible maturity—that of a *partnership with God*. We take responsibility to follow our inner wisdom, our inner calling. Whether we conceive God's will as the basic ecology of Mother Nature or the laws of a benevolent God, we surrender to a universal system that operates both within us and beyond our ego's power and understanding. When we surrender to God, we take responsibility for following and accepting God's will for us. We then act in the world and do what we are called to do. And by doing so we put ourselves on a track to heal our rift with God. There are no more deals to be made with God, only an ever-stronger relationship based on love, trust, and radical surrender.

FEAR OF THE NEW AND POWERFUL

Grace, one of my oldest and dearest students, is of the most loving and faithful spiritual aspirants you'll ever meet. She meditates and prays daily, performs selfless service, and brims over with spiritual joy. Filled with love, she treats all beings with compassion and reverence. Even spiders are safe in her care—she lets them build their webs wherever they want in her home but transports them outside with great care and respect if they build a little too close to her bed.

Making rapid spiritual progress, Grace had only one little crack left in her rift with God, but it stood out like the crack in fine china that everyone notices but no one talks about. She was afraid of the new and powerful Self emerging from her meek and mild persona. Everyone else could see it. When she read for us or stated her views on something we had said, we could feel the growing wisdom and spiritual power emanating from her. It was only when she spoke deprecatingly of her own abilities that we realized she did not see the power which we could see.

"Grace, I can't believe you're saying that," Julie told her one evening after Grace had confessed that she didn't feel "ready" to talk about spiritual growth to a local group which had requested it. "I listen to you here every week and I *know* you're ready. You're more than ready. You've got a lot to offer the world. What is your problem that you don't see it?"

Grace broke into tears and left the room, surprising everyone. Later, in private, she confessed that Julie's words had struck a wound that had haunted her for years.

"I know I have a problem with this personal-power thing, Paul, and I know it's confusing for people, but I can't help it yet. Whenever people have a need and I think about helping them instead of about my inadequacies, I can be strong and powerful and wise. I just feel God's love flowing through me, and I don't stop to question it.

"But that's not the way I see myself," Grace said, looking shy and forlorn. "When you ask me to fill a role as teacher, I freeze. I don't think I can do it, and a voice inside says, 'Who do you think you are? You don't know anything!' And I believe it.

"It's the same in my prayer and meditation. Often, after an especially powerful sitting, I feel a surge of spiritual force within, and I know it is from God. I feel confident and powerful, and I know I'm on the edge of something big, a power and role in life beyond what I can imagine. It scares me. I want to run away from it and not look back."

Grace was crying again, big belly sobs, the kind that shake loose mental structures if encouraged. I encouraged, asking Grace to let herself really feel that deep fear of her own power and potential. I knew from my own experience what she was feeling. Every step I've taken to new levels of spiritual unfoldment have been accompanied by the same fears, the same tears. I have pulled to the shoulder of a busy freeway on the way to give a speech and sobbed like Grace was at that moment. "Who do you think you are?" said the old self-image, the farm boy turned soldier turned factory worker. As I held Grace's hand and comforted her, I comforted myself and every lover of God who has unexpectedly confronted her own power.

Sometime or another on the spiritual path, as we slowly shift our identity from our relative personalities to our inner, cosmic nature, we will encounter a light and power beyond our previous comprehension. As the God of the Hebrew scriptures tells us, "Be still, and know that I am God." When we learn to still our minds, which tell us that we are merely limited humans, we gradually begin to realize our true nature as children of God. Jesus Christ told us over and again, "The kingdom of God is within you." And he said, "I in them, and thou in me, that they may be made perfect in one." Saint Paul reminded us again in the letter to the Corinthians, "Know ye not that ye are the temple of God, and that the Spirit of God dwelleth in you?"

But Saint John also said, "And the light shineth in darkness; and the darkness comprehended it not." We are more frightened by our light than by our darkness. We worship God, we pray to God, but when the moment comes to experience God's power and light as our true nature, we shy back, afraid of our own inadequacies. We are afraid of our own greatness.

How many people have I spoken with who told me that they avoided spiritual practice because of some powerful experience that shook them to the core? Far too many to mention! A fundamentalist Christian who had been "touched by the Holy Spirit," an American Indian woman whose intuitive abilities frightened both herself and her Caucasian friends, a meditator who faced the void of no mind and shunned meditating for years. Sometimes they admit to themselves that they were scared by this power, but more often they push it into unconsciousness because they have no context of understanding in which to place it. I had that same reaction to being hit by the light on that Christmas Day in Utah. I was both frightened and ignorant, and I "forgot" about the experience for months.

Grace's Solution to Power and Light

All of us in our spiritual community agree that if humble Grace can solve this issue of fearing our own power, anyone can. Gradually, as Grace realized that she has a job to do on this planet that can be accomplished only by one who accepts her own light and power, she began to find a solution. She began to consciously believe what the scriptures of most religions tell us, that we humans have a dual nature, both spirit and human. And she decided to let her human self do the human work and her spiritual Self do the spiritual work.

"It came to me in meditation, and I know it came from God," she explained in my office one afternoon. "I got real still inside and began to see the beautiful light that comes to me so often, and I began to feel myself expand as if to fill the universe. But when I started to contract from it in fear, I heard a voice say something like what Jesus said: "Of myself alone, I can do nothing. It's the Spirit that is within me that does the work." That's when it hit me: I am spirit, too. It's not my feeble little personality that's holding all this power and light, it's the Spirit that is within me. It's absurd for my personality to take credit for all of that. How egotistical! Of course. How many times have you guys been telling me that? I can do *anything* as long as I remember that it is the Spirit within me that does it. Wow! I'll teach the very next class that comes up."

Grace says it all, doesn't she? Today, she teaches classes at the local college and hardly bats an eye. She's confident and sure of herself because she realizes she is spiritual in nature. And a wonderful thing called integration has happened along the way. Her personality is getting the word, also. She is more confident and sure of herself in her daily life as well as in her spiritual life—which is a sure sign that she has really begun to heal her rift with God.

GAINING THE WORLD AND LOSING THE SELF

One of my saddest experiences in spiritual teaching is watching students routinely place their worldly concerns over their spiritual life. "But I don't have time for meditation (or prayer or spiritual reading)," they will say, so enslaved in the worldly mind that they sincerely believe they can't afford thirty minutes to bathe in the only waters capable of renewing their minds and setting them free.

Everyone I have ever taught has told me that when they have a strong spiritual practice such as meditation, their quality of life increases dramatically: stress lowers, relaxation increases, self-esteem increases. They feel much more free and at ease in life. Then comes the day when they stop their practice. They report that they simply got busy at work or into a new relationship and dropped their spiritual practice completely. And when they did, the suffering gradually began anew: stress increased, relaxation decreased, and self-esteem dropped. Most of us have experienced this process in ourselves at one time or another.

I believe Saint Paul's statement, "The fruit of the spirit is love, joy, peace, longsuffering, gentleness, goodness, faith, meekness, temperance." I have the personal experience of observing this truth work in my life and the lives of hundreds of others. *When we make our connection and time with God first, everything else in our lives works better.* This is why Buddha turned to the spiritual path and why Christ told us that he brings us a more abundant life—to relieve the suffering of humanity. Even a few minutes a day with God will improve our lives immeasurably. The only time I have seen this fail is when people try to manipulate God by attempting to cut a deal, as I described earlier.

Why does this simple lifestyle adjustment work so dramatically to transform our lives? I believe the answer to that question is quite simple: Spiritual work takes us inside ourselves, into the center of our being. Nothing can function well without a strong center. In the center of our being is our soul, our inner spirit, which is the internal command center for this immense cosmic being we call "myself." We cannot fully function from the ego, because the ego is externally referenced and extremely limited in scope. It doesn't know enough about us or our world to run the whole show for us. Letting the ego run our lives is like letting a letter carrier make policy decisions for the entire postal service. It simply doesn't know enough to run the whole operation.

When we take time to get quiet and go inside, we become aware of ourselves as a whole. We become aware of our thoughts, feelings, body sensations, level of stress, beliefs, assumptions, and attitudes. We become aware of when we're hungry and what we would like to eat, what we would like to do for a living, and what our being really needs for fulfillment. And if we are fortunate, we become aware of what the Quakers call "that still small voice within," our intuition and our inner wisdom, the only seat of authority with enough wisdom and under-standing to keep this immensely complex being healthy, fulfilled, and functioning meaningfully in the world.

This human being was not born to be a mere puppet on the mater-ial stage of life. We were born to greater things than making and hoarding money, lost in the illusion that things can make us happy. Our parents, schools, and societies taught us how to survive in the world, but they did not teach us to discover who we really are as unique expressions of divine consciousness. They did not teach us that we are at essence souls on a spiritual journey, much less how to discover and embrace them. They trained us to be fixated on the external world and how to survive in it. Important skills, to be sure. But by doing so to the exclusion of inner development, they turned our faces diametrically away from the only guidance system sufficiently wise and understand-ing to give us health on all levels, wholeness, integration, and fulfill-ment of our purposes here on Planet Earth.

Helping Lost Souls Find Home

When I meet a person who has begun to look within herself for the answers of life—whether through intensely contemplating herself, counseling, learning to meditate, joining a spiritual group, or turning to holistic health to find out how her own attitudes affect her health— I rejoice. By the same token, I feel saddened when I recognize in others the life choices I used to make, sacrificing health, happiness, and my soul's freedom for various types of achievement, falsely believing that money, things, and recreation could make my life work.

My friend and co-teacher Jim feels even more passionate regarding such choices. He has been an engineer for forty years, much of which he spent in the high-tech trenches of Silicon Valley. When he awakened from the external dream and turned within, he felt an overwhelming desire to go back to his old peers and call out, "You're going the wrong way! You're going the wrong way!"

"I really understand these people," he tells our group, "but that's because I was more obsessed with all that than most of them. I wanted tons of money and I wanted it fast. I worked faster and longer than anyone around me. I was there when they came in and there when they went home. I had it all: fast cars, great houses, women, fine food, booze, drugs. I worked hard and played hard. And I believed that all of it would eventually make me happy. Right up until my heart attack.

"It took a triple bypass to get my attention," Jim tells us. His eyes always get moist when he tells this part, a little sad for the pain but happy for the result. "I almost died, and that was enough to wake me up to the fact that what I had believed was the answer was not the answer to health and happiness in life. That's when I began my spiritual search, to look within myself for the answer.

"That's why it just breaks my heart to see these people lost in materialism and believing it's the answer to their suffering. They think it's in the car, house, 'the one,' or security. Most of them are like I was— not aware enough of their insides to *know* that they're suffering. I want more than anything to reach out to them, to get them turned around to find out who they really are. But most of them don't want to hear about it."

"For what is a man profited, if he shall gain the whole world, and lose his own soul?" asked Jesus Christ. "Lay not up for yourselves treasures upon earth," he said, "where moth and rust doth corrupt. . . . But lay up for yourselves treasures in heaven. . . . For where your treasure is, there will your heart be also." None of us, I think, can say it more clearly than Christ. Not even Jim, who, after almost losing his life to the outer system, is totally committed to showing others that "the kingdom of God is within." Incidentally, Jim makes more money now than he ever did. But not at the cost of his soul!

"Doing Our Job" for Soul Healing

A truly holistic approach to whole-being health tells us that all symptoms are unconscious aspects of ourselves trying to express—and that by becoming conscious of those aspects and helping them express, we can become more integrated and whole. My own experience with hundreds of students and clients suffering from a myriad of symptoms bears out this belief completely. We human beings are amazing and mystical in this vast complex act of becoming whole. We are here on this plane to become ourselves, that's very clear. But for the most part we have no idea who or what we are or what we are to become. Trained from childhood to behave as if our sole reason for being here is survival, we must evolve beyond survival and learn to see our purpose as much greater than that, far beyond our wildest dreams, if we are to honor our incarnation by healing our rift with God and becoming whole. We must understand that we are in the very act of co-creating with God our lives and the universe.

A very dear friend of mine, Angel, refuses to philosophize about her life and work. She has a very active life as a therapist and devotee of God, traveling thousands of miles yearly for therapeutic trainings and to see her spiritual teacher. She is very clearly far along on the path. But when asked about her vision of life, she says simply, "I just have to do my job." What is that job? "I don't think about that. I always know.

God may tell me through a pain in my back, a friend who is angry with me, or someone who needs my help. He may require me to stay and do what I'm doing, or to leave everything and move to some distant land. I don't know what is next, even now. Or what it will all mean in the end. Only by following this thread of my life wherever it leads me can I know my job."

I have no doubt but that this thread of her life that Angel follows is the impulse of her soul toward wholeness. *The most powerful and vital energy in the universe is the life force moving through creation to complete itself.* What else is there, really? And what are we but aspects of that life force in material form for a moment, here to become what we are meant to become? But our mind-bound state cannot conceive the vastness of this life force and cannot begin to glimpse the greatness of our destiny, interwoven as it is with the cosmic process and of all being everywhere. I believe our life's purpose is best served by learning, like my friend Angel, to find and follow our own thread of organic wholeness—to actively *do our job* rather than endlessly philosophize about it all.

It is my view that we are all on the same path. We are following that "thread of my life" that Angel described in our quest to heal our rift with God. Whether we are trying to find a mate, heal a symptom, find our right work, or heal our whole lives, we are seeking out our lost wholeness. And in the end we must acknowledge that we are at one with a mysterious universe called God that is busily going about the task of creating Itself. As vital parts of this cosmic creation, we can see how very important it is for each of us to cooperate with It, for when we do not cooperate with the will of our Creator, we place ourselves in opposition to Him. When we are in opposition to all creation, we can expect to encounter endless difficulties and suffering, but when we are in cooperation with our divine impulse, we find peace and love and grace. What better motivation than this to "do our job" in this cosmic process and heal our rift with God?

EPILOGUE

The Journey Continues

THE TWENTIETH CENTURY has been a time of integration, East and West, North and South, in science and practical living—and finally in medicine and philosophy. Spirituality, East and West, has traditionally emphasized a conflict between body and spirit, a sort of war in which spirit must overcome the body and its dark urges. Western medicine, for its part, has ignored the spiritual life—including the emotions, mind, and instincts—and treated the body as its scientific brethren have treated the earth and all civilization—as a mechanical problem to be solved.

With integration, all of that is changing very rapidly. The amazingly rapid shift of our culture into holistic health is forcing healers of all sorts to see us humans as we are: whole beings dependent upon integration, balance, and congruence of all our parts. *Healing Your Rift with God* is a child of that new understanding. It introduces my belief that our total well-being, indeed our health, happiness, and fulfillment, depends upon the integration of our lives with the will of the spirit within us and that the purpose of our lives is to learn how to find our rift with Self and God and to heal it.

Strange and magical are the ways of God and this unfolding universe! The events that have transpired in the past four years since I began this writing, and the amazing growth I have reaped from them, lead me to conclude this book with a short summary of these experiences. It is my hope that this story will aid the reader in seeing how we may detect our rift with God and how we may go about healing it, with results following. I also wish to demonstrate once again that God wants our wholeness and will continue to unravel our defenses against Him as long as our rift remains.

I might have known that the very act of writing a book of these immense implications—indeed, healing one's relationship with one's inner divinity—could turn my life upside down. It was, in a sense, a statement to God that I was willing to heal my own rift. After all, how can anyone but one who has faced the void and made at least some headway in the matter dare write about it? But for some reason, the thought that I might be asking for trouble hardly crossed my mind. As I look back, I'm amazed I didn't quake in my boots at the very thought of the days ahead of me.

To be brief, I have experienced more change, pain, and growth during these years than at any other time since my initial spiritual awakening, which I described in this book's introduction. In my professional life, very little seems to have changed. My financial outlook, which has always been of perhaps too little concern to me, has brightened. The two organizations I helped found have flourished, and I have felt increasingly full and comfortable as a minister, teacher, counselor, and healer. Those areas of myself, however, were already quite healthy and well developed.

Besides, being unattached to material outcomes has long been a major part of my spiritual practice. Like most mystics, I have taken Christ's advice quite literally: "Take no thought for the morrow: for the morrow shall take thought for the things of itself. Sufficient unto the day is the evil thereof." To truly heal the rift one must learn to trust God completely and do the work without worry for tomorrow. In that area of material nonattachment, I had made good headway. What was hidden to me at that time, however, by the comforts of marriage and my dedicated work on myself, was the tremendous attachment I had to a primary relationship: I thought I had completely healed the wound of abandonment that had incurred from my father's suicide. I was sorely mistaken.

The Loss of My Marriage

The first major event demonstrating this to me happened two years into the book. It was the dissolution of my marriage of fifteen years.

Although we had faced many challenges during our time together, my ex and I had thought we were in the marriage forever. But on the day that we knew it was over, a feeling emanating from my soul told me that this breakup was the right thing to do. Something our souls needed for the next stage of growth wasn't happening in our marriage, so it was time to let it go.

Knowing it was right didn't stop the pain of separation, of course. The loneliness and abandonment I felt were overwhelming. I have found that marriage can be a sort of cocoon for the emotions, protecting us from experiencing deep wounds from childhood, such as rejection and abandonment, and even that most primal of wounds, the sense of separation from God. Having someone who is bound by vows to be there for us, no matter what, gives us a secure feeling. But in my case, it was only a cover-up, a dependency on this other person to continue to prove, over and over again, that I was loved and safe and secure. The illusion left me when my wife left.

The greatest pain I felt came from the earliest wounds of childhood. I frequently found myself regressed to that time when my father died and I felt abandoned for being somehow inadequate and unworthy. I was certain that everyone else in my life would find me equally unworthy and leave as well. I felt these emotions anew, as if no time had elapsed at all since my father's death. I also felt despair. Would I never heal these wounds of childhood? I began to question my worthiness to write this book on healing the rift, since my own wounds were so resistant to healing.

But I and my friends were also very amazed to see how well I did during this period. I consciously and willingly experienced my pain as part of my spiritual practice, and I recovered very quickly. Each week brought surprising new growth and insight. To my surprise, I found I could live alone, manage a household and business, develop new friendships, and thrive as a single person. A year and a half flew by, and I was a divorced man. I was just beginning to congratulate myself for successfully recovering from divorce when the next storm hit.

Surprised by Love

I fell in love with an unattainable woman—from Europe, no less. We met at a seminar only two months after my divorce and the first draft of this book were complete. In some ways, we felt innocent victims of fate. We hardly interacted at this seminar until the very end, when we suddenly realized that we felt great love for one another. We both thought it ludicrous. In our only intimate conversation at the time, she told me that she was a God-surrendered and very happily settled mother and therapist who loved her home country and life's work there very much and was not open to relocating. And I told her that I was just recovering from a marriage and wasn't interested in a relationship at the time—and certainly not with a woman who lived five thousand miles away! This love we shared made no sense at all to either of us. And our individual spiritual guidance told us that this was not to result in a marriage. So we both returned to our separate homes with the firm belief that we had seen the last of each other. We thought we had control of our destinies.

The Fire of Spiritual Love

We both underestimated the fire of love that had revealed itself to us. I went home a confused mess. I didn't know what had hit me. A powerful energy began to course through my body day and night. It disturbed my sleep and kept me up till all hours. Yet with all that energy, I required very little sleep. Whenever I was alone, I would cry and pray uncontrollably, finding myself engulfed in both extremes of anguish and euphoria. I performed my work duties, teaching and counseling, very effectively, somehow protected from these passions. But when I was home alone, the tears and prayers would once again overcome me.

Finally, after some weeks, she phoned me. "What is happening to me?" she asked immediately, and she related the same symptoms I was experiencing. "I am still clear that nothing material will come of this. But I also know that what has happened to us is very important. It is a deep love, the kind of love I feel when I am closest to God. I believe

God has sent this love-fire to burn away all barriers between me and Him. But I don't know what I am doing or how to go about this. I must follow it with you, but we must keep it on a spiritual level! This is the right path—I know it. You must help me do this."

What a wonder it was to hear those words from her. What a miracle! As strange as this new concept of unattached love was to me, I knew she was right. As we communicated by phone and letter over the next few months, we found that our experiences were nearly identical. We felt a great love and passion for one another. We were obsessed, like teenage lovers. Yet at the same time, it was entirely spiritual. The more we connected, the more this torrent of fire flowed through us, opening up all wounds; destroying all old beliefs, attitudes, and structures; and leaving us raw and vulnerable. It also gave us a deeper feeling of God than we had ever experienced. God was in her; God was in me; God was in us.

It is impossible to express how much of an impact this made on our lives. She, of course, told her friends and family about this wonderful experience, as did I. To our surprise, we found a great deal of love and support from them. We were being given a powerful and wonderful gift from God—a transformative fire that was helping us heal our deepest wounds and bringing us closer to God than we had ever dreamed possible. My closest spiritual advisors were thrilled for me, telling me when I anguished over the situation, "The biggest mistake you could possibly make would be to not follow this to completion."

It was confusing to my personality and conditioned self, of course. My inner caveman thought I was absolutely crazy. To him, we were in love with a beautiful woman and should be trying to lure her to our cave and make her our life's partner. In the beginning, the caveman ruled my mind and thoughts quite frequently, bringing to the surface once again those old abandonment wounds of childhood that I thought were healed. And this time, it was worse than ever before. To love but not possess gave me a depth of pain I had not believed possible to feel and still survive. I even experienced the mind-numbing agony of my soul separating from God at the beginning of this life. The terror and suffering that went with this separation exceed my ability to describe.

I could only weep and sob, surrendering myself and my agony to God. I was forced to discover and develop new spiritual tools to help me survive this amazing spiritual process.

From the beginning, I and those friends close enough to know my secrets and spiritual life could see the great gift offered to me by having my lover be five thousand miles away. We were both very clear on the spiritual plane that the purpose of this love, for this time period, was spiritual healing and wholeness, not partnership. Yet all the passionate elements were there to fuel the fire. Had she been local or willing to relocate, we would most likely be married by now. There is no doubt in either of our minds that this is true. The love was too strong to resist. Our caveman and cavewoman would have made sure that the great healing agony of our love and separation would dissolve in passion and bliss.

But the distance between us and our deep commitment to our lives and work in our respective countries provided us with a sacred container in which to burn. Burn up all our old beliefs about what love is and what roles and structures must contain it. Burn away our false beliefs that we are separate from God. Burn up all illusions that we control our destinies. Burn away all resistance to total and unconditional surrender to God and our destiny as children of God. Though our love and passionate desire for each other was great, we soon learned that this spiritual burning and this unity we felt with God were far more important and fulfilling than what any physical partnership could give us. Our love is a gift of grace.

As I surrendered more and more to this transformative fire, I began to realize that I am being introduced to the feminine face of God. A man's soul is feminine, a woman's masculine. By falling so desperately in love with this amazing spiritual woman and not being able to possess her, I have been left with only the love. But what a love! She is my anima, my inner feminine, the archetypal Divine Mother. And by worshiping her—and worship is the correct word—I am worshiping the sacred sensual, the sacred feminine side of God and my Self. And this has given me an ability to love and nurture myself that I have never before known. Incapable of fully loving myself in the past, it was no wonder I needed others to love me in order to feel OK about myself.

In the agony and ecstasy of this love-fire, I was graced for a time with total union with God and could see clearly how little we control our fate and how ridiculous are our fears and worries. Like streams of water in the great river of life, we are intricately interconnected with all aspects of this great river and are being washed along our individual and collective paths of destiny whether we struggle or not. What worry or fear need we have? They are never helpful. Our only wise choice—ever—is to find out which direction this river is flowing and to flow with it, taking care to remain open and innocent, taking care to stay aligned with spirit in all things.

From this God-perspective, I also saw what God requires of us. And it's only those three things: the openness, innocence, and love of a child. A new mother brought her baby to our last spiritual retreat. As we meditated, prayed, and talked about God, the baby crawled around the floor, modeling the openness, innocence, and love that God wants of us. When he picked up a book or a key from the floor, he had no preconceived idea about that object; he did not dismiss it as "book" or "key."

"A little child shall lead them," said the prophet Isaiah of the Messiah. Yes. The child has no word or preconception for anything. Everything is fresh and new. Every moment is the only moment of his life. Everything is a great mystery. He is open and innocent, and therefore he flows in the great river of life without encumbrance. He basks in the adoration of all who behold him and beams back equal acceptance and love. God wants us to be like the child, because when we are, life is no longer difficult. And we no longer suffer.

When we are like the child, we follow Christ's teaching: "Take no thought for your life, what ye shall eat, or what ye shall drink; nor yet for your body, what ye shall put on. . . . Behold the fowls of the air: for they sow not, neither do they reap, nor gather into barns; yet your heavenly Father feedeth them. . . . Consider the lilies of the field, how they grow; they toil not, neither do they spin: And yet I say unto you, That even Solomon in all his glory was not arrayed like one of these. Wherefore, if God so clothe the grass of the field, which to day is, and to morrow is cast into the oven, shall he not much more clothe you, O ye of little faith?"

I have begun to understand that Christ was being quite literal when he said these words and so many like them. The child, like the lilies, is open and innocent. Unlike Adam and Eve, he has not eaten from the Tree and so he remains in the Garden, where God makes sure he is fed and clothed. And we on the spiritual path are called to that same openness and innocence of following the flow of God's will without "taking thought" for our lives. As Christ said, "Which of you by taking thought can add one cubit unto his stature?" Note that he did not say "unto his bank account," for we can do that. But money will add nothing to our real stature as humans or children of God.

Healing the Rift Continues

So now, as I complete this book, I see that I know far less than when I began it. In fact, the more I learn, the more I'm sure I know absolutely nothing. This great love continues, but with each day I know more clearly that it is not a mere woman I love so deeply and passionately, but God. We don't need to have an affair or get married, because our affair is with God, whom we see so clearly in each other. Our individual lives continue as before. We write and call and support one another with this love, which has not grown or abated one whit from the first moment it dawned upon us. We understand more clearly each day that it is a vast, spiritual love that came mysteriously out of the unknowable depths of God to burn us, bless us, and make us whole. And we are grateful beyond words for its coming.

For me, I feel at last a new stage in the healing of my rift with God. I know it will continue, this healing, till the moment of my death and beyond, but at last I know what it is like to love without fear of losing that love, to love without grasping, without the desperation for that "other" to prove my worthiness by staying with me and not abandoning me, as I felt my father had done. That constant fear of loss and abandonment is slowly receding from my nerves, fibers, and tissues. My body is relaxing more and more, and I often feel that absolute, overflowing joy which the masters tell me is my birthright. I am beginning to live in the center of love.

So, what has this experience taught me that can be helpful for the reader in healing her rift? Three things: (1) learn about and cultivate the openness, innocence, and love that God requires of us; (2) make your intention to know and follow God very clear, precise, and constant, repeating it and taking concrete and precise steps—such as those in this book—to follow through; and (3) do not hesitate to follow when God calls with an opportunity such as this great fire of love I have just described. No matter how ridiculous it may seem at the time, listen and follow and find out how it may transform your life.

Your opportunity will come in a different form from mine, because your wounds are different and you have different needs. Perhaps it will come in a business crisis, a death in the family, an illness, or sudden success beyond your dreams. But when that opportunity knocks, don't dismiss it out of hand because it doesn't fit your pictures, and don't turn it into something it is not simply to make it safe and familiar.

Be that little child with wide eyes who picks up the toy with great interest and enthusiasm. Feel it and shake it and smell it and hold it. Treat it like a gift from God, and then ask for the instruction manual. It may be just a toy to enjoy and later to return to its box. Or it may be that fateful divine gift which will at last help you on your journey to heal your rift with God.

RECOMMENDED READING

*Here's a short list of books that may be
helpful in healing your rift.*

Campbell, Joseph. *The Hero with a Thousand Faces*. Bollingen Series
XVII. Princeton, N.J.: Princeton University Press, 1949. A very
good text for learning the hero's journey.

Capra, Fritjof. *The Tao of Physics: An Exploration of the Parallels between
Modern Physics and Eastern Mysticism*. Boston: Shambhala, 1979. This
book is one of the major integrators of science and mysticism.

Carus, Paul. *The Gospel of Buddha*. Chicago: Open Court Publishing,
1915. A simple and sweet introduction to Buddhism that has
brought me joy.

Casteneda, Carlos. *The Teachings of Don Juan*. Berkeley, Calif.: University of California Press, 1968. The whole Don Juan series is helpful.

Davis, Roy Eugene. *God Has Given Us Every Good Thing*. Lakemont, Ga.:
CSA Press, 1986. This spiritual autobiography is a template for
spiritual living.

Dychtwald, Ken. *Bodymind*. Los Angeles: Tarcher, St. Martin's Press,
1986. A basic body/mind introduction. Very useful for beginners.

Eliade, Mircea. *Shamanism: Archaic Techniques of Ecstasy*. Bollingen
Series LXXVI. Princeton, N.J.: Princeton University Press, 1964.
An excellent introduction to mysticism without the religious
structures.

Feuerstein, Georg, trans. *The Yoga-Sutra of Patañjali*. Rochester, Vt.: Inner Traditions International, 1979. A most helpful guide to wholism, yoga style.

Grof, Stanislav. *The Holotropic Mind: The Three Levels of Human Consciousness and How They Shape Our Lives*. With Hal Zina Bennett. New York: Harper Collins, 1990. This book gives us a view and a map to wholeness.

Heisenberg, Werner. *Physics and Philosophy: The Revolution in Modern Science*. New York: Harper Collins, Torchbooks, 1962. A groundbreaking classic for the new thought. It may surprise you.

Jung, Carl G. *The Collected Works of C. G. Jung*. Bollingen Series XX. Translated by R. F. C. Hull. Princeton, N.J.: Princeton University Press, 1953–1979. Jung is the great integrator.

————. *Memories, Dreams, Reflections*. New York: Random House, Vintage, 1963. This is a must book for integrating science and mysticism, East and West, body and soul.

Kabat-Zinn, Jon. *Full Catastrophe Living: Using the Wisdom of Your Body and Mind to Face Stress, Pain, and Illness*. New York: Dell Publishing, 1990. This book ties together spiritual practice, health, body, and soul.

King James Version. *The Holy Bible*. Read mystically, the holiest book ever written. Read it again with new eyes.

Lao Tzu. *Tao Te Ching*. New York: Viking Penguin, 1963. Essential Taoism and an excellent guide to healing, spirit, wholeness, and life.

Lowen, Alexander. *Bioenergetics*. New York: Viking Penguin, 1975. A body/mind and energy classic. It is a guide for getting free.

Mindell, Arnold. *Dreambody: The Body's Role in Revealing the Self*. Boston: Sigo Press, 1982. This book opens a big door to healing the rift.

Mitchell, Stephen. *The Gospel According to Jesus: A New Translation and Guide to His Essential Teachings for Believers and Unbelievers*. New

York: Harper Collins, 1991. A helpful book for Christians trying to heal the rift.

Pelletier, Kenneth R. *Mind as Healer—Mind as Slayer: A Holistic Approach to Preventing Stress Disorders*. New York: Dell Publishing, 1977. Further study of the body/mind connection.

Prabhavananda, Swami, and Christopher Isherwood, trans. *Bhagavad-Gita: The Song of God*. Introduction by Aldous Huxley. NAL/Dutton, Mentor, 1944. This translation is easy to comprehend and apply.

Raheem, Aminah. *Soul Return: Integrating Body, Psyche and Spirit*. Lower Lake, Calif.: Aslan Publishing, 1991. This book, by one of my favorite teachers, is a must-read guide to whole living.

Shah, Idries. *The Sufis*. New York: Doubleday, Anchor, 1971. A wonderful introduction to the mystical world of the Sufis.

Wilhelm, Richard, trans. *The I Ching or Book of Changes*. Princeton, N.J.: Princeton University Press, 1950. A sacred text you must have on your desk or nightstand. One of my best friends and advisors.

Yogananda, Paramahansa. *Autobiography of a Yogi*. Los Angeles: Self-Realization Fellowship, 1946. This is a master's story. Read it.

Zukav, Gary. *The Dancing Wu Li Masters: An Overview of the New Physics*. New York: Bantam, New Age Books, 1980. A simple, concise guide.

OTHER BOOKS FROM
BEYOND WORDS PUBLISHING, INC.

DIVINE INTERVENTION
A Journey from Chaos to Clarity
Author: Susan Anderson;
Foreword: David Lukoff, Ph.D.; Afterword: Emma Bragdon, Ph.D.
$13.95, softcover

    Divine Intervention is a powerfully written and engaging story of spiritual transformation. Susan Anderson's journey from chaos to clarity provides hope and inspiration for anyone facing the challenge of a major crisis or life change. Susan's spiritual emergency causes her to reconnect with her true self and experience an authentic sense of fulfillment and joy that could only be created by a *Divine Intervention*. Having received rave reviews from doctors, spiritual leaders, and lay readers, this book is a treasure of insight and wisdom that will empower women and men to take charge of their lives. For those wanting to help anyone in a spiritual emergency, also included is a guide and resource directory by Emma Bragdon, Ph.D., author of *Sourcebook for Helping People in Spiritual Emergency*.

HOW MUCH JOY CAN YOU STAND?
How to Push Past Your Fears and Create Your Dreams
Author: Suzanne Falter-Barns
$12.95, softcover

    This is the little book of wisdom you've been looking for to steer you back on the path of your dreams. In fresh, funny language, *How Much Joy Can You Stand?* demystifies the creative process and gives you the inspirational kick in the pants you've been waiting for. Inside is all the reassurance and encouragement you need to get going and keep going. Stories, anecdotes, and the author's own hard-won wisdom tell the simple truth about creating your dream—that it's not as hard as you think, and you do, indeed, know exactly what you need to know. Find out where to find inspiration, how to handle rejection, whether talent really matters, and how to stick with your work even in the face of couch-potato attacks and complete creative meltdown. Hands-on exercises follow each short, pungent chapter to put you back on track toward achieving your goals. A One Spirit Book Club selection.

THE WOMAN'S BOOK OF DREAMS
Dreaming as a Spiritual Practice
Author: Connie Cockrell Kaplan; Foreword: Jamie Sams
$14.95, softcover

The Woman's Book of Dreams translates ancient teachings into a remarkable and life-changing spiritual practice for modern dreamers. It provides a profound yet simple system for tracking the thirteen types of dreams we experience and learning how to use them in our waking hours. *The Woman's Book of Dreams* also teaches how to chart dreams according to the cycles of the moon, the astrological information on the night of the dream, and the dreamer's biological cycles. This gives dreamers a personalized map whereby they can begin to see that on certain nights they can expect specific kinds of dreams: prophetic, telepathic, ceremonial, healing, shamanic, psychological, and spiritual. Also, through this tracking system, the dreamer learns how profoundly dreamtime impacts his or her daily life as well as how to become an intentional dreamer.

THE GREAT WING
A Parable
Author: Louis A. Tartaglia, M.D.; Foreword: Father Angelo Scolozzi
$14.95, hardcover

The Great Wing transforms the timeless miracle of the migration of a flock of geese into a parable for the modern age. It recounts a young goose's own reluctant but steady transformation from gangly fledgling to Grand Goose and his triumph over the turmoils of his soul and the buffeting of a mighty Atlantic storm. In *The Great Wing*, our potential as individuals is affirmed, as is the power of group prayer, or the "Flock Mind." As we make the journey with this goose and his flock, we rediscover that we tie our own potential into the power of the common good by way of attributes such as honesty, hope, courage, trust, perseverance, spirituality, and service. The young goose's trials and tribulations, as well as his triumph, are our own.

A LIFE WORTH LIVING
Recording Your Values, Memories, Goals, and Dreams
Author: Jerry Hawley
$19.95, hardcover

To provide a record of what each of us has done and where we are going, we created *A Life Worth Living*. The book is a living legacy for families to share for generations, and it includes pockets for mementos, blank pages to write affirmations, lots of questions for reflection, and an envelope for special treasures. Like Jimmy Stewart in the movie *It's a Wonderful Life*, few of us realize how our lives impact the people around us. Few of us record the details of our lives so that our children and grandchildren can know who we are, what has made our lives unique, who our friends are, what we have accomplished, and who touched our lives in memorable ways. Imagine the joy of discovering fascinating things about the lives of your parents and grandparents when you read what they have written in *A Life Worth Living*.

KINSHIP WITH THE ANIMALS
Editors: Michael Tobias and Kate Solisti-Mattelon
$15.95, softcover

Contributors to *Kinship with the Animals* represent a myriad of countries and traditions. From Jane Goodall illustrating the emergence of her lifelong devotion to animals to Linda Tellington-Jones describing her experiences communicating with animals through touch, the thirty-three stories in *Kinship with the Animals* deconstruct traditional notions of animals by offering a new and insightful vision of animals as conscious beings capable of deep feelings and sophisticated thoughts. The editors have deliberately sought stories that present diverse views of animal awareness and communication.

QUESTIONS FOR MY FATHER
Finding the Man Behind Your Dad
Author: Vin Staniforth
$15.00, hardcover

Questions for My Father is a little book that asks big questions—some serious, some playful, some risky. Each question is an opportunity to open, rejuvenate, or bring closure to the powerful but often overlooked relationship between fathers and children. Fathers have long been regarded as objects of mystery and fascination. *Questions for My Father* provides a blueprint for uncovering the full dimensions of the man behind the mystery. It offers a way to let fathers tell their personal stories and to let children explore their own knowledge and understanding of one of the largest figures in their lives. In rediscovering their dad, readers will discover themselves.

LOVE SWEETER LOVE
Creating Relationships of Simplicity and Spirit
Author: Jann Mitchell; Foreword: Susan Jeffers
$12.95, softcover

How do we find the time to nurture relationships with the people we love? By simplifying. And *Love Sweeter Love* teaches us how to decide who and what is most important, work together as a couple, and savor life's sweetest moments. Mitchell has warm, practical, easy-to-understand advice for everyone—young, mature, single, married, or divorced—interested in creating simple, sacred time for love.

HOME SWEETER HOME
Creating a Haven of Simplicity and Spirit
Author: Jann Mitchell; Foreword: Jack Canfield
$12.95, softcover

We search the world for spirituality and peace—only to discover that happiness and satisfaction are not found "out there" in the world but right here in our houses and in our hearts. Award-winning journalist and author Jann Mitchell offers creative insights and suggestions for making our home life more nurturing, spiritual, and rewarding for ourselves, our families, and our friends.

RITES OF PASSAGE
Celebrating Life's Changes
Authors: Kathleen Wall, Ph.D., and Gary Ferguson
$12.95, softcover

Every major transition in our lives—be it marriage, high-school graduation, the death of a parent or spouse, or the last child leaving home—brings with it opportunities for growth and self-actualization and for repositioning ourselves in the world. Personal ritual—the focus of *Rites of Passage*—allows us to use the energy held within the anxiety of change to nourish the new person that is forever struggling to be born. *Rites of Passage* begins by explaining to readers that human growth is not linear, as many of us assume, but rather occurs in a four-part cycle. After sharing the patterns of transition, the authors then show the reader how ritual can help him or her move through these specific life changes: work and career, intimate relationships, friends, divorce, changes within the family, adolescence, issues in the last half of life, and personal loss.

CREATE YOUR OWN LOVE STORY
The Art of Lasting Relationships
Author: David W. McMillan, Ph.D.; Foreword: John Gray
$21.95, hardcover; $14.95, softcover

Create Your Own Love Story breaks new ground in the crowded and popular field of relationship self-help guides. *Create Your Own Love Story* is based on a four-part model—Spirit, Trust, Trade, and Art—derived from McMillan's twenty years' work in community theory and clinical psychology. Each of these four elements is divided into short, highly readable chapters that include both touching and hilarious examples from real marriages, brief exercises based on visualization and journal writing that are effective whether used by one or both partners, and dialogues readers can have with themselves and/or their partners. This book shows readers how they can use their own energy and initiative, with McMillan's help, to make their marriage stronger, more enduring, and more soul-satisfying.

THE INTUITIVE WAY
A Guide to Living from Inner Wisdom
Author: Penney Peirce; Foreword: Carol Adrienne
$16.95, softcover

When intuition is in full bloom, life takes on a magical, effortless quality; your world is suddenly full of synchronicities, creative insights, and abundant knowledge just for the asking. *The Intuitive Way* shows you how to enter that state of perceptual aliveness and integrate it into daily life to achieve greater natural flow through an easy-to-understand, ten-step course. Author Penney Peirce synthesizes teachings from psychology, East-West philosophy, religion, metaphysics, and business. In simple and direct language, Peirce describes the intuitive process as a new way of life and demonstrates many practical applications from speeding decision-making to expanding personal growth. Whether you're just beginning to search for a richer, fuller life experience or are looking for more subtle, sophisticated insights about your spiritual path, *The Intuitive Way* will be your companion as you progress through the stages of intuition development.

To order or to request a catalog, contact
Beyond Words Publishing, Inc.
20827 N.W. Cornell Road, Suite 500
Hillsboro, OR 97124-9808
503-531-8700 or 1-800-284-9673

You can also visit our Web site at *www.beyondword.com* or e-mail us at *info@beyondword.com*.

BEYOND WORDS PUBLISHING, INC.

Our Corporate Mission:

Inspire to Integrity

Our Declared Values:

We give to all of life as life has given to us.
We honor all relationships.
Trust and stewardship are integral to fullfilling dreams.
Collaboration is essential to create miracles.
Creativity and aesthetics nourish the soul.
Unlimited thinking is fundamental.
Living your passion is vital.
Joy and humor open our hearts to growth.
It is important to remind ourselves of love.